Imagine a World

Pioneering Black Women Sociologists

Delores P. Aldridge

UNIVERSITY PRESS OF AMERICA,® INC.
Lanham • Boulder • New York • Toronto • Plymouth, UK

Copyright © 2009 by
University Press of America,® Inc.
4501 Forbes Boulevard
Suite 200
Lanham, Maryland 20706
UPA Acquisitions Department (301) 459-3366

Estover Road
Plymouth PL6 7PY
United Kingdom

Library of Congress Control Number: 2007943308
ISBN-13: 978-0-7618-4004-6 (paperback : alk. paper)
ISBN-10: 0-7618-4004-4 (paperback : alk. paper)
eISBN-13: 978-0-7618-4187-6
eISBN-10: 0-7618-4187-3

To my colleagues who have been generous with their patience for the release of this portrayal of pioneering Black women in the sociology for change.

To the Black women sociologists who are not in this publication but whose lives will be illuminated in a forthcoming larger volume.

To my students who have participated in discussions of the lives and works of these women and especially to those who read a draft of the current manuscript in my course on Race, Gender and Social theory offered in Spring, 2007.

In memory of two of the women who are no longer with us:

Dr. Vivian V. Gordon

Dr. Jacquelyn J. Jackson

Contents

Preface

As African American women in the post-emancipation era, Anna Julia Cooper and Ida Wells-Barnett framed social theory under conditions of radical social change which they personally experienced and placed in socio-historical contexts. While they were not intellectual colleagues, that is, they did not have sociological conversations or did not discuss pressing issues of the day, they responded to the same critical experiences in African American history. In the early 1890s, each published significant social thought—Cooper, the book-length collection of essays entitled *A Voice for the South* (1892), and Wells-Barnett, two major research pamphlets, *Southern Horrors* (1892) and *A Red Record* (1895).

Though not employed in the academy, Cooper and Wells-Barnett provide a sociological analysis of society as a dynamic of power and difference, a theory as complete and critical as any achieved in American social science–a radical, non-Marxian conflict theory, as the race factor, not a part of the Marxist paradigm, is so pronounced in their works. These women focus on the pathological interaction between racial difference and power in the USA, a condition they variously label as "repression," "domination," "suppression," "despotism," "subordination," "subjugation," "tyranny," "our American conflict." Of the two women, Anna Julia Cooper occupies an extremely unsettled place in the early tradition of African-American social thought. This is because she has only recently been more widely acknowledged as a contributor to that arena of ideas. Although a focus of substantive discussion in the past two decades in literary studies and African-American intellectual history (Carby, 1987, Gaines, 1996, Giddings, 1984, hooks, 1981), Cooper has only recently been more thoroughly recognized as a significant contributor to social thought. This was due, in large part, to references to her in numerous sociological works (Blackwell and Janowitz, 1974; Hill-Collins, 1991; Lengermann and Niebrugge-Brantley, 1998) and the republication of Cooper's major work, *A Voice From the South*, originally published in 1892, together with a collection of her essays and correspondences (Lemert & Bhan, 1998). Cooper produced most of this work prior to receiving a PhD in Sociology in 1925 from the Sorbonne in Paris. She was 66 years old when she received the degree.

The lack of that degree did not prevent her from setting forth ideas that are now being recognized as precursors to much of the contemporary sociological debates on African-American womanhood. Rather than engage in any consistent form of data collection, Cooper wrote critical essays that examine the situation of African Americans in the public domain and in the home. Moreover, Cooper connected the socio-political circumstances concerning and affecting African American men and women to those of the USA more generally. She argued that the ever increasingly complex industrial order in the society would reach its fullest potential only by including African American men and women into the citizenry and allowing them to participate fully in the social, political, and economic dimensions of life.

A Voice from the South includes discussion of sexual exploitation—a phenomenon that, at the time of her writing, was still decades away from achieving mainstream legitimacy in debates about gender relations and social justice, class differences, gender-specific education, and other issues that remain at the forefront of debates on the social status and prospects for African Americans today. In advancing her claims, Cooper was balanced in her perspectives on women in that she emphasized the home front as a particularly legitimate space for women in general, not only Black women. Likewise, there was advocacy for women to have roles in the political arena and be formal agitators for social progress. Her life experiences, including the rearing of seven children (five of whom were adopted) as a single parent, the founding and management of a school in Washington, DC, and the constant interchange with Booker T. Washington and other African American civic leaders and spokes persons, was the best empirical example of the social theory that she espoused.

Whereas Cooper's scholarship took the form of critical essays and commentaries, Ida Wells Barnett introduced empirical approaches toward uncovering certain problems and concerns for African Americans. She was born in 1862 and wrote extensively in the late 1800s for the newspaper, *The Memphis Free Speech*. As a journalist, Wells-Barnett was even farther removed professionally and socially from academia than was Cooper. Yet, her efforts resulted in the first substantive account of how social analysis could inform public understanding of important social issues and events. More specifically, Wells-Barnett (Harris, 1991) provided a keen analysis of the sociological foundations for the lynching of African Americans. In the course of her career as a journalist, she prepared statistical accounts of the phenomena, which, as one should imagine, were extremely hard to document. Those accounts, together with data that she amassed while studying the involvement of white women in civic and social organizations that served the African American community, helped her challenge the public notion that lynching was a justifiable response to sexual assaults suffered by white women at the hands of African-American men. Not only did Wells-Barnett demonstrate that occurrences of such assaults were not as common as had been believed, she also demonstrated that the argument itself was a technique used by whites to sanitize the practice of lynching (Carby,1987 [1892]). This is an early example of social analysis applied to racial practices.

Wells-Barnett also argued against the exclusion of African American women from the analytical debate on womanhood that was a part of the chivalrous culture of the nineteenth century South. Altogether, her work resulted in a strong theoretical association between racism, sexism, and classism as it existed in southern social relations in the post bellum era. Both Wells-Barnett and Cooper precede the scholarship usually regarded as the beginning of an African American sociological tradition. Yet, each actually introduced the two ends of the continuum, critical commentary on the one hand and empirical investigation on the other, that shaped contemporary sociological inquiry. As African American women with no formal place in the academy, Cooper and Wells-Barnett were left on the margins of an already marginal constituency in American sociological thought. Importantly, while many of today's feminists point to both of these women as being precursors of Black feminism, neither of these women engaged in acts that could be considered gender specific. Rather, their work clearly indicate they were also engaged in a race based struggle for the liberation of their people, a position strongly taken and pointed out by more contemporary scholars (Hudson-Weems, 1993 and Gordon, 1985). The focus on gender and race might categorize them as humanists concerned with the rights of all groups irrespective of race or gender. Importantly, the efforts of Cooper and Wells-Barnett, though not of the academy, set the stage for six of the most politically engaged and radical women sociologists of the twentieth century, women who imagine a world different than that which exists. All of these women's lives can be captured by the notion of scholar-activist or public intellectual or scientist in community, as each imagines the kind of world she envisions. All are concerned with meaningful research, research which specifically challenges dominant White perspectives and White cultural hegemony. In the world they imagine, relevant research on Black people will receive wide dissemination that is linguistically and stylistically accessible to both the sociological community and beyond.

Acknowledgments

This book is the result of several years of teaching race, gender and social theory; and race and cultural democracy in a wide array of university courses and other settings. I would like to thank all the students in those classes who quickly made it clear to me the importance of educational insights which emerge from such interfaces of intellectual ideas.

In particular, I want to thank Pavel S. Blagov, Tiffany N. Davis, Kazumi Hasegawa, Molly K. Larson, Terrence K.S. Oliver, Brenda D. Tindal and Adria N. Welcher. Each read and made valuable comments on this project and it is better for their contributions. My colleagues Rutledge Dennis, Sandra Taylor, and Obie Clayton have each contributed to insights into the works of the Black women sociologists who are highlighted in the volume. Most especially I want to thank Clenora Hudson-Weems who read the entire manuscript as someone outside of the discipline of sociology or the social and behavioral sciences. But, who had a keen eye for editing.

I also want to thank my publisher, University Press of America, for advice and wisdom particularly at the final stages of publishing the book. And finally, many thanks to Katie Wilson for painstakingly typesetting the appendices.

Introduction: Six Women Scholars in the Framing of Social Theory and Social Change in American Sociology

In the summer of 1988, Critical Sociology published an issue focusing on the emergence of the "Sociology Liberation Movement" in the late 1960s (Oppenheimer and Murray). These "radical sociologists," predominately white, called for a shift from an allegedly objective, though actually conservative, sociology to a sociology that would include a subjective component, dedicated to positive social change—thus, paraphrasing and rephrasing Robert S. Lynd's question, "Knowledge for What?" into a "Sociology for Whom?"

Members of the "Sociology Liberation Movement" argued that sociology should be a tool for social change as opposed to a science merely utilized to leverage and support the power elite. Accounts of the "Sociology Liberation Movement" by the advocates of this campaign reflect the view that they, via their insistence on a politically-engaged stance, would be on the cutting edge of change.

A close reading of the history of "engaged-sociology" would acknowledge that a politically-engaged stance has been a hallmark of Black social thought for nearly a century, as captured by Anna Julia Cooper and Ida Wells Barnett and illuminated by W. E. B. DuBois. Three decades before Robert Lynd asked "Knowledge for What?" and six decades before the rise of the "Sociology Liberation Movement," W. E. B. DuBois saw sociology as a tool in the struggle against racism as did Cooper and Wells-Barnett, though perhaps not discussed in texts as such. DuBois' vision as reflected in his 1968 autobiography characterizes sociology as a vehicle for social change and reform which is examined in the lives and works of six Black women sociologists in this book. Historically, the vast majority of scholarly works has been the product of Black male sociologists and there are largely gender issues to explain the paucity of female sociologists within the sociological sanctuary (See Jackson, 1974).

While recognizing Cooper and Wells-Barnett as early "engaged" social theorists, Black women entered the academy and gained recognition within the discipline later than Black men, and they continue to be less visible in the discipline. Like male sociologists, many of their female counterparts have approached sociology from a politically-engaged perspective. This book explores the contributions of some, not all, of the most active and productive female sociologists to the discipline and to the larger society. For this reason, we want to know about the theories and issues which propel and inspire them in their role as sociologists. We propose to address this gap in the literature by exploring the ways in which six prominent and contemporary Black female sociologists—Jacquelyne J. Jackson, LaFrancis Rodgers-Rose, Joyce A. Ladner, Doris Wilkinson, Delores P. Aldridge, and Vivian V. Gordon—demonstrate the connections between social change, sociology and the issues and policies which guide their approaches to their sociology and their society.

"Most studies concerned with women as professionals ignore blacks, and most studies concerned with black professionals ignore women" (Jackson, 1975, p. 267). As Jackson illustrates, it is not for a lack of their presence and productivity within the discipline. Black women in particular, as well as other individuals who have succeeded and produced in spite of the barriers they have faced within and without academia, may be considered even more remarkable than those who have simply produced (Epstein, 1973).

Any study of Black female sociologists must, of necessity, analyze the ways in which Black females: 1) "do" sociology, and how these differ from the manner in which even Black males as well as White male and female sociologists "do" their sociology. That is, what is the unique perspective brought to the sociological table by Black female sociologists? 2) A conjoint question must extend to "why" this particular sociology is different; and, 3) What does this different sociological perspective mean for sociology as a discipline, the manner in which Black communities relate to and with each other, and the ways in which this Black female sociological perspective expands/broadens our sociological knowledge-base to such a degree that social change and social reform would become realities.

As we discuss each of the sociologists presented here, we want to emphasize how each person represented has contributed to what C. Wight Mills (1959) called "the sociological imagination." It will be the distinctiveness of each sociologist presented in this volume that will enable us to verify the uniqueness of a black female sociological perspective. Mills contended:

> The sociological imagination enables its possessor to understand the larger historical scene in terms of its meaning for the inner life and the external career of a variety of individuals. It enables him to take into account how individuals, in

the welter of their daily experience, often become falsely conscious of their social positions. Within that welter, the framework of modern society is sought,
and within that framework the psychologies of a variety of men and women are
formulated. By such means the personal uneasiness of individuals is focused
upon explicit troubles and indifference of publics is transformed into involvement with public issues (p. 5).

Mill continues

. . . We have come to know that every individual lives out a biography, and that
he lives it out with some historical sequence. By the fact of his living he con-
tributes, however, minutely, to the shaping of this society and to the course of
its history, even as he is made by society and by its historical push and shove
(p.6).

In sum, the sociological imagination enables us to grasp history and biography and the relations between the two within society. That is its task and its
promise. To recognize this task and this promise is the mark of the classic social analyst (p.6). Mill pushes the social scientist toward clarification and so-
lution of our most pressing present-day problems. Thus, the sociologist would
"do" sociology by being engaged as the pioneering black women sociologists
in this work.

SOCIOLOGY FOR WHAT? AND SOCIOLOGY FOR WHOM?

Sociologists who view a career in academia have traditionally focused on
three primary tasks as they seek to build and sustain their professional careers: 1) to publish original research; 2) to teach (where their jobs require it);
and, to provide service to their departments, universities and professional associations. Individuals building academic careers in sociology need not produce knowledge relevant to social change or empowerment. Instead, they are
required to produce knowledge that responds to gaps in existing academic literature — knowledge which may or may not actually be useful in the world
outside of academia. Further, sociologists are neither required to be active,
nor expected to be active in non-academic organizations, activities, and/or
employment. In fact, some scholars would argue that such involvement taints
the sociologist's objectivity and thus actually harms her/his career. In sum,
the sociological "establishment" has neither required nor encouraged politically-engaged scholarship.
　　Jacquelyne J. Jackson, LaFrancis Rodgers-Rose, Joyce A. Ladner, Doris
Wilkinson, Delores P. Aldridge, and Vivian V. Gordon are six unique and

nationally known sociologists who will be highlighted in this volume. We want to chart their histories and sociologies and to ascertain the special directions of their sociological research which they have used as a tool for social change. In each case, we will be able to see their intellectual and academic evolution as they built their careers in the discipline. Original work by each of these pioneering women is appended for direct scrutiny. The important experiential bases of each will demonstrate how one brings questions and focus to careers from one's lived experiences. In addition, we will be able to understand how these sociologies broadened the very definition of the sociological enterprise by their movements between academic sociology and non-academic organizations, various social movements, and non-academic employment. The features of these sociologists aid in our understanding of how each in her own way remains true to historic politically-engaged scholarship which has been central to Black Sociology.

Chapter One

Jacquelyne Johnson Jackson
"New Age Policy Advocate"

> . . . Minimum age eligibility for retirement benefits should be racially differentiated to reflect present racial differences in life expectancies.
>
> —Jacquelyne Johnson Jackson

Jacquelyn Johnson Jackson, a daughter of the South, born in Winston Salem, North Carolina, reared in Tuskegee, Alabama in a time when both dejure and defacto segregation were the norms, knew well what it meant to be "different" from the larger society. Though she and her twin sister, Jeanne Naomi Penn, were born into what many would consider "polite black society, both parents being professionally trained, the sisters were black females growing up in a racist south in the 1930s.

Jackson's concerns regarding race were always at the forefront of both her academic and nonacademic life. A sociologist and civil rights activist, she earned her undergraduate and Master of Arts degrees from the University of Wisconsin and her doctorate from the Ohio State University. Jackson was an associate professor of medical sociology at Duke University Medical Center from 1968 until her retirement in 1998. After retiring, she moved to be close to her daughter's family in Stillwell, Kansas where she died on January 28, 2004 at the age of seventy one.

Prior to taking the position at Duke, she held teaching positions at Southern University in Baton Rouge, Louisiana, Jackson State University in Jackson, Mississippi and later at Howard University in Washington, DC. She had also held a research appointment at Duke University, Durham, North Carolina. As founder in 1970 of the National Caucus of Aged Blacks, Dr. Jackson was active in political affairs, particularly in minority issues in the Research Triangle in North Carolina and throughout the nation. Among the many affiliations with organizations focusing on the aged were the Committee on aging, National Academy of sciences and the Task Force on economic Security for Older Americans, Council on Church and Society, United Presbyterian Church, USA.

For many years she was a member of the Board of Trustees of the Carver Research Foundation of Tuskegee Institute and received numerous fellowships and awards including the Solomon Carter Fuller Award from the Committee of Black Psychiatrists of the American Psychiatric Association, the W.E.B. DuBois Award from the Association of Social and Behavioral Scientists and an award for Outstanding Service from the President's Advisory Council on Equality of Educational Opportunity.

Nationally recognized expert on ethno-gerontology and racism, she was the author of numerous works on aging, with special emphasis on minorities. In addition, she researched in other areas of social concern. She was the first African American to edit a journal of the American Sociological Association. She is listed in the Ebony Success Library, Notable Black American Women and Whose Who Among African Americans. She pioneered the study of aging in Black Americans as a post-doctoral fellow at Duke and is included in the 1976 Bicentennial photographic essay, *Living Legends in Black America,* by J.E. Bailey which was displayed at the Smithsonian Institute.

Jacquelyne Johnson Jackson's primary academic and political focus is on Black aging. Her early interest in gerontology was grounded in a concern with the potential usefulness of gerontological research in conjunction with race and inequality. In a 1975 article, "Aged Blacks: A Potpourri in the Direction of Reduction of Inequalities" she writes:

> Among the earliest gerontological papers on black aged were probably three first appearing in *Phylon*. Since then, such papers have multiplied, but this proliferation has failed to produce sufficient interest in improving the objective social conditions (e.g. income, housing and transportation) of black aged, nor has it aided those experiencing involuntary relocation in the onslaught of urban renewal and highway programs. These are serious problems (1975:36)

This passage indicates the macro issues influencing Jackson's interest in social change. It also raises an important question: if existing academic knowledge has failed to be a catalyst for change in the lives of these women, what choices does a politically-engaged sociologist have? She could then decide that sociological research in and of itself is inherently useless in the struggle for new developments (as W. E. B. DuBois did later in his life)—this would lead her to abandon research and become a full-time activist. She could then decide that sociological research is indeed the most important source of societal change, if done correctly—and thus concentrate solely on producing socially relevant research for changing institutions within the society. Finally, she could decide—as Jacquelyne Jackson apparently did—to combine research and activism into an almost unified whole.

Jackson's edited volume Aging Black Women: Selected Readings for NCBA (1975) is a case in point. This anthology was published by the National Caucus on Black Aged (NCBA), an organization "particularly concerned about dramatizing and reducing those significant gaps characteristic of services to, training for, and research about black aged. . .Its most immediate missions [in 1970] are a) dramatizing the plight of aged blacks; and b) having a significant impact upon and input into the forthcoming 1971 White House Conference on Aging" (Jackson, 1975: 376–77). Jackson was active in the organization and served as director and chair for its third annual conference on "Aging Black Women and Federal Policies: 1960–2000 A.D." in 1975. She also became the Executive Director of NCBA in 1975 and continued in this role for many years.

Aging Black Women is a compilation of relevant research on societal issues "developed to provide related background material for participants" in the 1975 conference (Jackson, 1975: 3). In the introduction, Jackson notes that liberation is a key theme in many of the articles in the collection. In addition, the articles address four main concerns of the conference: Black women and economics; Black women and education; elderly Black women; and Black women and health (ibid.) Jackson ends the introduction with the following comment: "we hope that [the collection's] extreme fragmentation and other shortcomings will be recognized as a microscopic condition of the available work about Black women, and researchers will be encouraged to reduce these unnecessary gaps by helping to upgrade generally the statuses of aging Black women" (1975:7). This comment highlights Jackson's belief in the importance of empirically grounded and socially relevant research.

Jackson's dual concern with rigorous empiricism and social relevance is particularly evident in her own research in Aging Black Women. In a study titled "Aged Negroes: Their Cultural Departures from Statistical Stereotypes and Rural Urban Differences," she argues that little empirical research has been done on aged Blacks and that such information is vital to the success of programs serving this population (1975:359). She then focuses on Census data to reveal specifics about this population that defy existing "statistical stereotypes" about the Black aged. In the midst of this academic discussion of Census and other data, however, Jackson suggests policy changes.

Jackson recommends that "minimum-age eligibility for retirement benefits should be racially differentiated to reflect present racial differences in life expectancies" because most Black people "(a) die earlier, (b) perceive themselves as being 'old' earlier, and (c) are in fact, old earlier than are whites"(1975:360). Jackson then moves to an analysis of rural-urban differences between Black aged, returning again to policy recommendations at the end of the discussion. One such recommendation reads: "it is incumbent upon the federal government to continue to improve its program, planning and evaluation for such aged. Moreover, it is even more incumbent upon the federal government to encourage the local, county and state governments . . . to begin (or to upgrade if they have begun) to plan and activate realistic and humanistic programs for their aged" (1975: 363).

The tendency to move back and forth between rigorous statistical empiricism and policy recommendations is evident in many of Jackson's other writings in the collection as well; "Aged Blacks: A Potpourri in the Direction of the Reduction of Inequalities" (quoted earlier in this section) is a particularly strong example. Jackson begins this research with a detailed study on Black grandparent-grand-child relationships, moves from there to policy recommendations regarding housing and telephone services for aged Blacks, and then goes on to a case study of NCBA. She concludes the study with a carefully argued recommendation that the minimum eligibility age for a specific old-age government insurance program (OASHDI) be lowered for Blacks. Jackson explains the connection between the three foci of the article as follows:

> The grandparent data point toward the need for improved economic and housing conditions for grandparents, for their children, and for their children's children. The National Caucus on the Black Aged is significantly concerned about improving these adverse conditions . . . The specific proposal to realize greater racial equality between aged whites and blacks [in terms of OASHDI] is one response to the need to improve the deplorable income plight of many Black aged" (1975:384).

Jackson ends the article with the comment that she hopes that her "paper will play a small part in contributing towards the gradual increase in effective research, adequate training, producing increased personnel, and above all, meaningful services available to aging and aged Blacks (1975:385).

Jackson's attention to the connection between empirical research and social relevance is also evident in her work as Project Coordinator for the Ministerial Training Program in Eldercare to At-Risk Black Elders (MTEARBE) from 1992–93. As the project coordinator, Jackson produced The MTEARBE Black Church Manual on Eldercare for AT-Risk Black Elders in Pitt County, North Carolina (1993). This document combines demographic information on Black elders with information on public policy (the Older Americans Act and its provisions for programs and services to older adults) and a list of agencies in Pitt County providing services to older adults.

In the introduction to this manual, Jackson: 1) begins with an argument for the importance of church involvement in caring for Black at-risk elders and moves to a discussion of the statistical information available in the manual; 2)The discussion includes comments on the importance of statistical information as well as the reliability and validity of the data involved; 3) She concludes with a call for volunteer-based referral services and simplification of the bureaucracy of existing governmental programs for elders. Although her primary focus is on aged and aging Black people, Jackson has published scholarly articles on a variety of other topics as well. Two of these articles in particular reflect Jackson's trademark connection between rigorous empiricism and social relevance.

In "But Where are the Men?" (1971), she uses statistical data to dismantle a variety of negative academic and political myths about Black women–including the myth of their greater educational advancement, the myth of their employment advantages and the myth of these women as matriarchs. She then points out the low Black male-to-female sex ratio, arguing that female-headed families are a realistic and intelligent adaptation to numerical reality.

In 1974, Jackson provides a critical update from the point of entry to the early 1970s of Black females into the sociology profession with her work on the topic. This study appeared as a chapter in a volume on black sociologists edited by Blackwell and Janowitz. She employed a methodology which included personal experiences and observations, library research and mailed questionnaires. In exploring previous studies of Black sociologists, Jackson concluded that the most impressive finding drawn from her examination was the absence of any concern about women, as evidenced partially by the general failure to separate the data by sex. Pointing to the dearth of data available on Black female professionals, she investigates the characteristics of these social scientists—one of which is a greater likelihood of engaging in research focusing on problematic considerations affecting Blacks (1974:286). She calls for greater development and utilization of the "older" pool of talented sociologists, arguing that such a strategy "could well be a major factor in improving significantly our knowledge and understanding of Blacks and Black-White relationships in the United States" (1974:287). Both of these articles reflect her embracing empirically rigorous and politically engaged research that has the potential to facilitate positive empowerment of the groups with which research is conducted.

Much of Jackson's non-academic political work is tied directly to her research on aging (and vice versa). However, there are two exceptions to this rule: her very poignant letters-to-the-editor to the Herald Sun in Durham,

North Carolina and her work with the Federation for American Immigration Reform (FAIR). While a few of Jackson's letters-to-the-editor in the (Durham, N.C.) Herald-Sun emerge from her research expertise, (e.g. a letter on racism and Social Security, 11/29/94: A8), many others go beyond the scope of her published work. Topics include: the county commissioners' response to the murder of a young girl (Jackson, 10/28/94: A12), the O. J. Simpson trial (Jackson, 10/6/95: A10), and county funding to a local non-profit organization (Jackson, 10/16/94: A14).

Jackson has been vocal about other controversial issues such as those involving the influx of illegal immigrants and their impact on the Black community in the United States (Hyer, Washington Post, 12/24/80). Her comments merited consideration and received wide dissemination. She later served in 1993 as a member of the national advisory board of the Federation for American Immigration Reform (FAIR). Jackson was "unsettled" when FAIR accepted a donation from the notoriously racist Pioneer Fund (Ferriss, San Francisco Examiner, 12/12/93: A-1).

Even with the lack of data, which one expects in a letter, Jacquelyne Jackson's use of sociology as a tool for change reflects a deep commitment to an interrelationship between rigorously empirical sociological research and socially relevant policies. The link between Jackson's research and her politics is particularly evident in her research on Black elders and her work with NCBA and MTEARBE. How related or unrelated are Jackson's multiple roles—as activist and academic—in her day-to-day life? How intertwined do these multiple roles feel to her? The answers to these and other questions are areas for further research. But, what is clear is that "doing sociology" for Jackson is to actively integrate theory with precise even when treading the waters can prove to be highly controversial.

Chapter Two

La Francis Rodgers-Rose "Myth Buster: The Science of Mass Appeal"

". . .individual and collective beliefs (i.e. myths about blacks) affect and sometime even create reality. Sociological research, then, can only impact reality in as much as it reaches people."

—La Francis Rodgers-Rose

La Francis Rodgers-Rose comes from a history of struggle. Growing up in segregated Portsmouth, Virginia with her mother, two older brothers and a younger sister, she experience riding in the back of the bus, drinking from the "colored" water fountain, and attending segregated schools and movies. Rodger-Rose stated in an interview with the writer that "Seeing the full spectrum of American segregation shaped her comprehension of the world and its power relationships." Her mother held different jobs at various times to care for her family–domestic worker, beautician, licensed practical nurse, insurance agent, and waitress. At an early age, she thought she would become a lawyer, having asked one of the few black lawyers in her hometown what his major was in college. He told her sociology, a field she, too, started out in, but she never left.

Rodgers-Rose graduated from Morgan State University in 1958 with honors in sociology and anthropology, and from Fisk University where she participated in Civil Rights activities. She attended the University of Iowa where she focused on social psychology with her dissertation being an empirical test of Harry Stack Sullivan's theory of interpersonal psychiatry. In 1964, she accepted her first full time teaching position and since that time held various positions. In 1972, she left academia for a position at Educational Testing Services (ETS) in Princeton, New Jersey. She was concerned with improving services at a time when the controversy regarding race bias in aptitude testing had begun to emerge and become quite heated. She left the position because of differences in direction from those of her own and returned to teaching. From 1973–1988, she held a part time teaching position at Princeton where she offered the first course on the Black woman in 1974. Finding nothing in the field of sociology that spoke from the voices of black women, Rodgers-Rose embarked on a mission to create the first textbook that could be used in the social sciences about black women, by black women, from their own perspective. The result was the classic work, *The Black Woman* an edited volume published by Sage Publications in 1980. The book became a best seller going through eleven printings.

Like Jacquelyne Jackson, LaFrancis Rodgers-Rose's work reflects a concern with the production of socially relevant knowledge, as does the work of all the subsequent women to be discussed. While Jackson focuses on the institutional level (e.g. changes in government policies affecting Black elders and Black religious institutions' interactions with their elders), Rodgers-Rose focuses on the individual and cultural levels.

> In the preface to her well-known anthology *The Black Woman*, Rodgers-Rose argues that the knowledge of the history of Black women tells us that they continue to live in an oppressive society . . . as we move into the 1980s, we find that Black women must continue to remember, to be, and to relive the slave and peasant existence of their ancestors. To do so means that the African-American woman will never be separated from her reality. This is not easy, since her history has not been readily available to her" (1980: 10).

According to Rodgers-Rose, Black women's historical memories are one of the keys to their empowerment in a society which has not encouraged or promoted their full participation.

Rodgers-Rose also points out that dominant White culture is waging a battle to redefine Black women. Television, for example, presents a distorted view of the realities of Black women's lives. Biased research conducted by social scientists is another part of the problem. "For the most part, these social scientists have been white, they have not lived the experience of Black womanhood, nor have they made an earnest effort to be introspective learners and observers" (1980: 11). Rodgers-Rose also acknowledges and supports Black social scientists' research challenging dominant views about and images of Black people. However, she notes that research supporting dominant ideas about Black people receives much more publicity than research challenging those ideas. The former are likely to have a greater impact on the general public.

In the context of a struggle over who will define Black women's history and day-to-day realities, Rodgers-Rose writes that *The Black Woman* is a volume that "seeks to continue theprocess of correcting the history of Black women. It aims to go beyond the debunking of the prevailing ideology. . .the underlying purpose in each of these essays is a quest for the reality of the situation" (1980: 12). The volume is organized by special topics. The first section focuses on social demographics; the second on Black women and their families; the third on the impact of political, educational and economic institutions; and, the final section examines Black women's behaviors from a social psychological perspective. "We hope," writes Rodgers-Rose, "that this volume will shed light on what it has meant and continues to mean to be a Black woman in America . . . If we have caused the reader to think, reflect and evaluate in any way the Black woman in America, our efforts were not in vain" (1980: 13). From Rodgers-Rose's perspective, sociology is one of the tools that can unearth the realities of Black women's lives. Dissemination of such knowledge can affect understanding; this in turn can facilitate positive movement in changing their social, economic, and political conditions within the society.

True to her focus on culture and her interest in accurate historical information, Rodgers-Rose's first piece in *The Black Woman* focuses on Black women's history. Her historical account points to the strength of Black women's West African cultural history and to the ways in which that cultural legacy survived and changed during slavery. She points out that strong mother-child bond, strong work orientation and independence are all West African cultural traits that endured during slavery. And, while these values may have been held by other cultures, it is important to underscore their importance as West African values so as to eliminate any questions of values passed on to Black people in the USA. Above all, writes Rodgers-Rose, "Black women survived . . . they continued to work along with their men, struggling as best they could to assure the survival of their children (1980:21). From this perspective, Black people's survival and transmission of their culture make social change possible. Families function in part to transmit culture and pass along memories to children. It is no surprise, then, that Rodgers-Rose is concerned with the strength of Black people's familial relationships–particularly Black male-female bonds.

According to Rodgers-Rose, the Census data that Jackson used reflected an undercount of Black men as opposed to an actual shortage of them. Though demographic data supported Jackson's sex ratios, Rodgers-Rose argues that, contrary to Jackson's analysis, the Black male-female sex ratio is not particularly skewed. The problem, she argues, is the recent (in 1980) increase in marital discord between Black husbands and wives. Rodgers-Rose points out that the economic, political and educational institutions of the United States "are affecting Black women in such a way that the very survival or continuation of the Black family is being threatened. Without the survival of the family, that of our Black children is impossible. Unless our children can survive, both physically and mentally, we as a people cannot survive" (1980: 40).

Are survival and change of the social conditions possible and can social science research facilitate the process? Rodgers-Rose's approaches to Black male-female relationships indicates her belief that the answer to both questions is "yes." From her perspective, changing the lives of men and women will take place at the individual and cultural level and academic research is atool that can either facilitate or hinder such change. Therefore, Black social scientists must conduct accurate research on Black people and disseminate the resulting information.

Rodgers-Rose points out that (in 1980) "most of what we know about Black male-female relationships is a result of biased research conducted by white social scientists": (1980:251). She argues that this biased research leads to destructive myths about Black male-female relationships. These include the myth that Black women have led or dominated Black men; the myth that Black men are shiftless; the myth that Black women have an economic advantage over Black men. Also, included are the myth that Black women emasculate Black men; the myth that Black children have no male role models, and the myth that Black men and women are innately sexually aggressive towards white people (1980: 252–3). According to Rodgers-Rose, Black social scientists should uncover and correct flaws in existing research "before we can move toward defining Black male and female relationships, we must expose false definitions that grow out of those systems which serve to divide and conquer Black people. To the extent that we are unaware of these false reality systems, we will believe them, define them as real and . . . they will become real in their consequences" (ibid.).

Rodgers-Rose contends that individual and collective beliefs affect and sometimes even create reality. Sociological research, then, can only impact the reality inasmuch as it reaches people. We live within a system, however, in which research challenging dominant White perspectives of the world does not receive wide dissemination. Further, traditional sociological research is often linguistically and stylistically inaccessible to most people, but it is accessible to thesociological community. Since Rodgers-Rose's research focus suggests that cultural transitions and new social processes must occur first at the individual level of knowledge and belief. Because this is such an important first step, it was essential for her to broaden her audience on this research. For this reason, Rodgers-Rose explains, she began conducting workshops (with her brother, Dr. James Rodgers) on resolving conflict in Black male-female relationships.

Unlike published academic articles, community oriented workshops reach beyond the academy. However, their impact is limited to those people who are actually able to attend. Therefore, Rodgers-Rose and her brother released a book based on tapes from the conflict resolution workshop (Rodgers-Rose and Rodgers, 1985). By moving her work partially outside of the traditional sociological arena, Rodgers-Rose widened its impact. This impact is suggested in a 1993 biographical note which mentions that Rodgers-Rose "has appeared on national television and is a very popular national speaker" (biographical note in Aldridge and Rodgers-Rose, 1993: 165).

Co-edited with the present author, Rodgers-Rose's anthology, *River of Tears: The Politics of Black Women's Health*, highlights another facet of her concern with action research and new developments at the individual and cultural level. In this case, the focus is on Black women's health. Rodgers-Rose's concern with health is also reflected in her work as President and Founder of the International Black Women's Congress. *River of Tears* emerged from presentations and conversations at that organization's fifth national conference in 1989. The International Black Women's Congress was founded in 1983 as an international, non-profit networking organization comprised of women of African descent from around the world.

The fact that *River of Tears* is directly connected to Rodgers-Rose's leadership in a non-academic organization and to that organization's annual conference is reminiscent of Jacquelyne Jackson's *Aged Black Women* collection for NCBA. However, *Rivers of Tears* is far less academic in tone than is *Aged Black Women*. The approach makes sense when we consider the different audiences for the two collections—Jackson's compilation was targeted to researchers and policy makers, while *River of Tears* was compiled for Black women, particularly the younger generation. In their introduction to the volume, Rodgers-Rose and Aldridge write that *River of Tears* is a collection of much needed data and available resources on Black women's health by Black women. As a result of a broad range of stories, data and resources, young Black women may be in a better position to understand and alleviate some of the issues surrounding their health care, making way for another generation of Black women whose tears will be of joy and the triumph of justice in a structurally unjust society (1993: 10).

Rodgers-Rose's article in *River of Tears* points to the deteriorating health of the Black population. The following passage from that article reflects her continued interest in history, culture, individual-level improvements and the need for different approaches in the future:

We need to examine closely the beliefs, values and behaviors of our foremothers. We must return to our source, to our rich African heritage in order to help us survive the racism of 21st Century America. "An enculturated Black" will not survive . . . we should know that nothing in American society was designed for

us. No one has ever cared about our health but us. We cannot afford to leave the
well-being of a million of African-Americans in the hands of a system that . . .
over a course of nearly 400 years has been responsible for more than 30 million
deaths of African-American men, women and children . . . we must return to our
source; we must reclaim African healing systems. We must reflect, reconsider
and implement those things that are right for us . . . [If we do this] we will be
stronger and we will shape the future (1993: 14).

Overall, LaFrancis Rodgers-Rose's use of sociology as a tool for action research demonstrates a deep concern with the survival and well-being of Black
people, and a connected belief that Black people themselves must be at the
center of social action. This perspective highlights the need for sociological
research that is accessible to people who are neither professional academics
nor members of the "power elite," which is consistent with the belief of other
women discussed in the volume.

Does Rodgers-Rose believe that her work *has* reached a large audience?
Does she feel that she has suffered any loss of academic status with her choice
to write and present her research in accessible language? Or, how important
was/is academic status to her? The answers to these and other questions also
have implications for further research. But, more important, Rodgers-Rose as
an engaged social scientist grounds her "doing sociology" in social psychological, cultural and historical frameworks. And, like Jackson, who is ever the
gerontologist and political sociologist, Rodgers-Rose transcends the notion of
Black women scholars "dealing with race relations" removed from a broad
range of social science approaches. Rodgers-Rose, like other women in the
volume, have chosen to focus much, if not all, of her work on Black people
because such work is the most meaningful they wanted to pursue in doing
their sociology. The focus of their work and "their world," as DuBois put it —
"his world would be Black people—" this focus does not minimize the reach
of their grasp into varied arenas any more than white scholars focusing on
"their world."

Chapter Three

Joyce A. Ladner "Seeing the Glass Half Full and Other Radical Notions"

"It is only when the analysis of the oppressive forces which produce various types of anti-social behavior has been conducted that we can reverse the conceptualization of pathology. The society, instead of its members, becomes pathological."

—Joyce A. Ladner

Joyce A. Ladner was born and reared in Hattiesburg, Mississippi into a working class family. She and her sister, Dorian, were always very close, sharing many of the same perspectives on race relations in the South. In 1964, Joyce A. Ladner received a Bachelor of Arts degree in sociology from Tougaloo College in Mississippi. In 1966, she received a Master of Arts degree in sociology from Washington University. Her master's thesis was entitled "Deviance in the Lower-Class Adolescent Sub-Culture." She received a Doctor of Philosophy degree in sociology from Washington University in 1968. Her dissertation was titled "On becoming a Woman in the Ghetto: Modes of Adaptation." From 1968 through 1979, she was an assistant professor of sociology and curriculum specialist at Southern Illinois University in Edwardsville, Illinois. In 1969–1970, she served as a Senior Research Fellow at the newly established Institute of the Black World (IBW) of the Martin Luther King Center for Nonviolent Social Change (King Center) where she was on the cutting edge of African-American scholarship.

Ladner's connection with IBW was significant because it signaled an affinity with a leading and innovative "Black Power" think tank. In 1970–1971, she was a Post-Doctoral research associate at the University of Dar es Salaam in Tanzania where her husband served as the US ambassador. During her African period of study, she had the common experience of reconnecting with her ancestral homeland according to conversations with her. Her African study reflected her heightened black consciousness that was acquired at IBW. Her scholarly contributions have focused on the following areas: African-American female socialization; teenage pregnancy; cross-racial adoption; history of sociology; race and ethnic relations; and poverty.

SCHOLARLY WORK

Of the six sociologists discussed in this essay, Joyce A. Ladner writes most openly about the tension between her own values and those of traditional sociology. In the introduction to her dissertation-turned-book, *Tomorrow's Tomorrow* (1971), she writes:

> Having been equipped with the deviant perspective in my academic training, yet lacking strong commitment to it because it conflicted with my objective knowledge and responses to the Black women I was studying, I went into the field with a set of preconceived set of ideas and labels that I intended to apply to these women.

This, of course, meant that I had gone there only to validate and elaborate on what was *alleged to exist*. . .However, this role was difficult, if not impossible for me to play because all of my life experiences invalidated the deviant perspective. As I became more involved with the subjects of this research. I began to perceive my role as a Black person, with empathy and attachment . . .on the one hand, I wanted to conduct a study that would allow me to fulfill certain academic requirements, i.e. a doctoral dissertation. On the other hand, I was highly influenced by my Blackness—by the fact that I, on many levels, was one of them [her subjects] (xiv, italics in original).

Acutely aware of the "double consciousness" DuBois has written about, Ladner felt compelled to choose sides. Was she a social scientist or was she a Black woman who happened to be a sociologist? After "a considerable amount of agonizing self-evaluation and conflict over 'whose side [she] was on,'" Ladner concluded that at one level, she was "unable to resolve the dilemmas [she] faced as a Black social scientist because they only symbolized the larger questions, issues and dilemmas of our times' (ibid.). Nonetheless, she did make a choice: " I decided whose side I was on [her subjects] and resolved within myself that as a Black social scientist I must take a stand and that there could be no value-free sanctuary for me" (1971: xx).

In opposition to the dominant racist focus on the pathology of Black families, Ladner decided that her "primary concern [in *Tomorrow's Tomorrow*] is with depicting the strength of the Black family and Black girls within the family" (1971:xxi). In *Tomorrow's Tomorrow*, Ladner also sought to highlight the systems-level racism permeating U.S. society. Her dual focus on Black women's strength and systemic racism allowed her to re-evaluate stereotypes of Black girls and women. In opposition to the idea that poor Black children are deprived of a "healthy and normal" childhood, Ladner argues that social and behavioral scientists should view these children differently. She insists that they "view the Black child, whose life has been an unrelenting series of harsh experiences, as a more emotionally stable and well-integrated personality than his white counterparts, whose protected, sheltered lives are representations of the most fragile personality the society can produce" (1971:49).

In opposition to the idea that racism causes Black women to hate themselves, she asserts that "many of these young ladies possessed an abundance of human resourcefulness and hope for improving their life chances. Any hatred, if present at all, was directed towards those individuals and institutions which inflict pain upon them, instead of being inflicted inward" (1971:77). Ladner acknowledges that the Black girls in her study did engage in behaviors deemed "anti-social" by the larger society. In her discussion of one such behavior—stealing—she points to the feelings of deprivation among young Black girls living in a racist society, concluding that "it is only when the analysis of the oppressive forces which produce various types of anti-social behavior has been conducted that we can reverse the conceptualization of pathology. The society, instead of its members, becomes pathological" (1971 "101"; italics in original).

Ladner's focus on the pathology of societal racism also permeates her discussion of "illegitimacy" and premarital sex. She points out that with all of the concern about "illegitimate" children among Blacks, "it is interesting that the children of white, middle-class white women are not referred to as 'illegitimate' or 'bastards,' but are called 'love children'" (1971: 238). Similarly, she notes that Black women who engage in premarital sex are seen as loose and promiscuous, while the same behavior by white girls prompts sex education in the schools and an institutionalization of the sexual revolution. "While this [sex education, etc.] is a very healthy sign, it only mirrors the fact that the majority group had to sanction the behavior before it became legitimate" (ibid.).

In the context of her discussion of the pathology of racism in the United States, Ladner stresses the importance and potential impact of social movements:

> As a Black person committed to social change, I refuse to surrender the last glimmer of hope for the hundreds of thousands of Black men, women and children

who appear to have lost incentive to continue to strike out against oppression. Many seem to be finding that sorely needed motivation and hope within various organizations which are designed to encourage political expression and also enhance one's feeling of power over his (sic)destiny. . .This trend was started on a broad scale in the 1960s with the advent of civil rights movement and the war on poverty, and will continue, on greater scale, in the decade of the seventies (1971: 176, italics from original).

Although she does not discuss her own involvement in the civil rights movement (*Newsweek*, 11/12/79:49) in *Tomorrow's Tomorrow*, Ladner's commitment to grassroots activism was likely affected by her work in that movement and her other race conscious building experiences mentioned earlier. The Civil Rights Movement also facilitated the emergence of a "Black sociology" that was openly critical of traditional white sociology. Ladner was clearly a part of this movement within the discipline. In 1973, she edited an anthology titled *The Death of White Sociology*. She refers to this collection as "an early statement on the statement on the development of Black sociology" (1973: xxvii). Sections in *The Death of White Sociology* include: "The Socialization of Black Sociologists"; "The Social Victimization of Black Americans: A Critique"; "Black Sociology: Toward a definition of Theory"; "Black Psychology: A New Perspective"; Toward a Black Perspective in Social Research"; "Subjective Sociological Research"; and "Institutional Racism: Two Case Studies."

The "Sociology Liberation Movement" mentioned at the beginning of this book had several institutional centers, one of which was Washington University. In 1968, Joyce Ladner received her Ph.D. in sociology from this university. Given Ladner's politically-engaged stance, it is somewhat puzzling that Henry Etzkowitz's article on "radical sociology and the fate of radical sociologists at Washington University" in the late 1960s does not mention Ladner at all (Etzkowitz, 1988: 95). Her 1968 dissertation turned book was published approximately 16 years before his publication.

Etzkowitz does note Lee Rainwater's study of the Pruitt-Igoe community (a project Ladner assisted) but does not mention Ladner's dissertation research (leading to the publication of *Tomorrow's Tomorrow*), which focused on that same community. Rutledge Dennis notes that Rainwater's study, "to an extent, reports themes already made by Daniel Patrick Moynihan (1965) in his assessment of Black family life. The litany of marital conflict, interpersonal discord and sexual initiations is a consistent thread throughout [Rainwater's book]." Ladner's study, on the other hand, "relates to all the contradictions and ambivalences Blacks in general, and Black women in particular, encounter in trying to deal with their realities. There is the pain, but there is also the joy, there is aloneness but there is also the togetherness. The conclusions drawn from the Ladner study is such a sharp contrast to the . . . Rainwater study that one might wonder if they were really studying the same people in the same housing complex" (Dennis, 1988: 35).

In *The Death of White Sociology*, Ladner notes that "certain white sociologists have challenged [sociology's] traditional roles by establishing the Union of Radical Sociologists" (1973: xxvi). However, Etzkowitz's omission of Ladner in his article and Dennis' description of the Rainwater study indicate that some "radical sociologists" were themselves partially replicating the racist themes of traditional sociology. Even in the supposedly liberated 1960s and 1970s, Ladner and other Black sociologists were writing in an academic and political context in which racism pervaded even the more progressive wings of white sociology. One of the ways in which Black scholars, including Ladner, responded to this pervasive but unexamined racism was by developing alternative analyses of life in poor Black communities.

In a 1986 article titled, "Black Women Face the 21st Century: Major Issues and Problems," however, Ladner argues that Black scholars' response to academic and political racism may have obscured important social problems. For almost 20 years following the publication of the Moynihan Report, Black scholars devoted considerable time to producing an alternative body of scholarship which sought to depict the strength, coping skills and overall positive aspects of black family life. However, the strong emphasis on strengths of black families as well as an attempt to minimize the seriousness of teen pregnancy and the rapid increase in female-headed households may have unwittingly led to an exacerbation of these problems. This is not to suggest that an early sounding of the alarm by scholars would have solved these problems. Obviously, the root causes are deeply embedded in the social structure and are closely linked to the transformation of the economy and conservative social policies leading to a dismantling of the welfare state (1986: 14).

Also, there is no evidence of Ladner's earlier faith in grassroots social movements in this article. Instead, she recommends that teen pregnancy should be prevented via school-based health clinics, school retention programs, state-mandated sex education and coordination of services. She offers several recommendations for eliminating Black female poverty. These include: creating new enterprises to serve as a transition to full-time jobs for females who receive public assistance; and, targeting funds for females enrolled in two-year colleges. She also suggests establishing coordinated education and training centers linked to specific industries; and, diversifying the types of jobs and industries in which Black women are employed. Finally, she notes the need to restructure welfare to support family stability and to create policies and structures that enforce child support payments (1986: 18–19).

What were the factors that led Ladner to de-emphasize or possibly lose her faith in grassroots movements? How did Ladner's work in the Civil Rights Movement affect her Scholarship in sociology? Was her appointment as Howard University's first female interim president (Jet, 6/694: 5) and her subsequent termination from that post (Jet, 7/10/95: 11) connected to this trajectory? And if so, how? Her subsequent appointment to a commission to deal with educational issues in Washington, D.C. followed by several years tenure as a senior fellow at a think tank in the same city are important benchmarks in her professional career and bare exploration into "her sociology". Whatever conclusions are reached, like all the women in this volume, Ladner is a politically engaged social scientist who "does sociology" her way. Ladner, a deeply passionate social scientist decries the value-free stance long taken by sociology. "Doing sociology" is for her, a mix of micro and macro theory translated into action to change the social conditions that foster the marginalization and negative portrayal of those of African descent. Again, the center of her world, relevant study and projection of Black people, as is that of most white scholars, focus on and about white people.

Chapter Four

Doris Wilkinson "Fighting Words: The Creative Intellect as Weapon"

The term 'minority' should be eliminated from academic research, public policy and journalism largely because of its inexactness. . .(The word) diminishes individual personalities and devalues unique heritages. It is a word of political convenience promoted by those in power.

—Doris Wilkinson

Among the contributions of African American women to the discipline of sociology include the impressive work of Doris Wilkinson. A valedictorian and Phi Beta Kappa member, Professor Wilkinson received the Ph.D. in medical sociology from Case Western Reserve University in 1968 at a place and time when Black women receiving terminal degrees in this area was unheard of. She also received the M.A. in Sociology from Case Western Reserve in 1960. Having committed her career to transforming the discipline of sociology and accepting the views of Black sociologists, she became the first African American to be officially elected to the Council of the American Sociological Association (Blackwell, 1992) and the first African American female to occupy the Vice Presidency of the ASA. which distinguishes her as an intellectual of great versatility.

Wilkinson's research career largely entails foci on issues of race meanings, gender and ethnicity. A listing of her publications shows an examination of research that spans themes from interracial dating and marriage to Black women and the segmented labor market. She has also published in the areas of the African American male, caregivers and the elderly, and racist/capitalist theories. Important contributions are her analyses of key institutions, including the effectiveness of Black colleges and universities to issues in health and medicine. Her essay on the role of race, class and gender in framing health policy is a classic (1987: 140–144).

Wilkinson's many pursuits in research training have well-prepared her for critical discourse and analysis. Most recently, she discusses the concept of "minority" as a term that should be eliminated particularly in the areas of academic research, public policy and journalism largely because of its inexactness (*Journal of Sociology and Social Welfare*, 2000). Wilkinson sees the term as being virtually useless and explains that it diminishes individual personalities and devalues unique heritages. She views it as a word for political convenience that is promoted by those in power. Because the concept has been used to refer to different racial and ethnic populations including white women in the workplace, multiracial and biracial persons, unemployed individuals, white Appalachians, those in the inner-city or on reservations, gay men and lesbians, and those with mental and physical challenges, there is even more reason to eliminate the term according to Wilkinson.

In reframing the language of the social sciences and of policy makers so that "minority" is replaced with a more precise and meaningful concept, Wilkinson states that "to be referred to as a "minority" is a disadvantage to those in such groups" (Turner, 2000). She notes that the American power structure has a vested interest in retaining the usage of the term, "minority" and that it functions to lump rejected individuals in the same social category. While her argument is not completely new, it is provocative and more clearly articulated. Within the academy today, however, this important "movement" to discontinue a scientifically used word tends to be based on national practicality as opposed to contemporary intellectual discourse. Accordingly, "it has sound implications for policy formation and acceptance of the legitimacy of racial and ethnic history and ancestry and group choices for how such populations should be identified" (Wilkinson, 2000). This current practical and intellectual "movement," especially within the area of cultural and ethnic relations, is underway and gaining momentum. It emphasizes eliminating the term for racial populations from all writings, research, policy, government documents and public discourse.

Wilkinson's probing of the racial connotations linked to the term and the need for its elimination is critically argued and rooted in research as evidenced in her published works, many of which are found in the bibliography. To her, the change is necessary in order to enable groups with definite cultural, economic, and political histories, specific and constitutionally shared demographic characteristics, genetically and geographically linked ancestries, and common family ties to be identified as they choose. Otherwise, "minority" is a "hodgepodge" that lumps a wide range of individuals thus becoming confusing and belittling. She documents the fact that "there is so much contrast between the ethnic traditions and lifestyles of the different groups lumped together as "minorities" as to render the word useless (Turner,

2000). She further notes that people are who they are, and not what they are purposefully labeled and that "they should be identified (specifically) by their race or ethnic background, which is no less important than recognizing them by their gender or sexuality" (Turner, 2000).

This type of well-developed and sound argument is not novel to Wilkinson who has a reputation for presenting challenging viewpoints and taking principled stands when less confident scholars would rather remain silent. For example, Wilkinson authored the first review essay by a social scientist to challenge the "happy and contented slave" theme and the thesis underlying Herbert Gutman's *The Black Family in Slavery and Freedom, 1750–1925* (Wilkinson, 1978). This book, published in 1976, the same year as the publication of Alex Haley's *Roots*, was well received. It uncovered flaws in the reasoning about the nature of slavery in the United States.

ON GENDER

Wilkinson's work in gender, particularly in relation to race and ethnicity, is well-known. An intriguing article published in *Daedalus* (1995) on gender and social inequality documents the role of race as a perpetual factor in enhancing parity for women. This important critical essay represents a new interpretation of the implications of the classic, *An American Dilemma*, and highlights the theoretical and practical implications of interpreting gender within a racialized social environment.

Wilkinson has maintained a pedagogic role throughout much of her career and this is reflected in her compiling much resource materials, as with some of the other women in this work, particularly Aldridge and Gordon who will be discussed later in the book. Wilkinson compiled and distributed at the Annual Meeting of the American Sociological Association, August 2000, a teaching-research resource, entitled, "Race Conscious African American Women Scholars: Selected Writings." This useful resource bibliography includes selected essays and books by leading women writers and scholars in the social sciences, humanities, and in law who recognize the significance of race in the social order and political culture. A focus on the study of writings that appear in this compilation exemplifies a major part of Wilkinson's concentration areas. Earlier she established the first African American Studies Program at the University of Kentucky and served as its first director from 1992–1997. Another area of her research on the interaction of race and gender includes a social history analysis of the segmented job market. At the beginning of the 1990s, she articulated a critical historical reinterpretation of the labor force participation of women in the 1890s and has studied women in today's labor market. A similar classic work (Aldridge,1974) had been presented by another pioneering woman social scientist whose work will be discussed in a later chapter. Another area of gender research for this warrior woman has been the African American male. Among other topics related to black masculinity, she has written extensively about the socialization process and characterizations and identities of the African American male (1977, 1980).

ON RACE

Other work for which Wilkinson has won national recognition include her views on racial identity. She has long argued against the application of arbitrary labels to persons, documenting the historically based stigmas often associated with such labels. Recognizing that multiculturalism and ethnic diversity characterize U.S. society, Wilkinson champions a move toward giving self-recognition and individual privilege to citizens to decide how they want to be racially classified. A now popular question of progressive scholars, Wilkinson long ago raised the question of "Who shall decide how a population should identify itself?" Her work on racial identification coincided with the U.S. Census Bureau's plans to include a "mixed race" category for self-identification. In 1990, while a visiting professor at Harvard, Wilkinson wrote an informative and critical essay on racial self-identification that was selected as the "landmark article" for that year by the journal, *Society/Transaction*, journal based at Rutgers University.

Wilkinson's work has gained recognition in the national community of major scholars and political leaders. The aforementioned article titled, "Americans of African Identity," Published in 1992 was among 32 works published in *Society,* one for each year since the journal's founding in 1963, considered as the most significant articles of the years in which they appeared. (Other authors whose works have been chosen for *Society's* top honor include former Supreme Court nominee Robert Bork, former U.S. representative to the United Nations, Jeanne Kirkpatrick, and Russian writer Aleksandr Solzhenitsyn.)

While Wilkinson understandably rejects the term "minority," (as previously presented), she holds that the concept of "race" is useful. She contends that "race" is a functional analytic tool and heuristic device, a position rejected by a number of scholars. Nevertheless, in the area of medical sociology, the utility of "race" as a valid concept is being examined increasingly in studies on health and disease entities (See Wilkinson and King, 1987). Of interest, however, are the number of courses throughout the country that have changed from "race and ethnic studies" to "cultural and ethnic studies." This may represent, however, a "politically correct" and post-modernistic movement that de-emphasizes the interests of Black people. Although the argument for the elimination of "race" as a valid concept abounds, Wilkinson holds to the position that "race" (unlike "minority") is useful in social and economic analysis and in everyday life. This contention is clearly seen in her insightful and instructive social history treatise on race in the social structure (Wilkinson,1999). While some of the previous discussion may have led the reader to assume Wilkinson is in conflict with the women from the earlier chapters who insisted on the "survival" of "Black" and on the importance of studying race as a category, to the contrary she places value on race as a relevant factor for social analysis.

In her probing analysis, Wilkinson reviewed the history of racial classification for those of African descent born in the United States. African Americans and suggested changing "Black" to "African American." Prior to and following the recognition of her national acclaimed essay on Americans of African identity, she participated in intellectual forums on nomenclature and how classifications shape lives. She has been an articulate voice about labeling phenomenon providing thorough explanations of the functions and politics of identities. Spanning the spectrum from "Colored" to "African American" to "People of Color" with identities of Black and Afro-American in between, Wilkinson has eloquently elaborated on what all of this means for people's self understanding and for policy for people of color.

ON CLASS

Research and discourse on class issues have also been prominent in Professor Wilkinson's intellectual agenda. She has written about poverty, inequality, justice and injustice, violence, race and racism, gender, and other issues related to class. She has also discussed the science of sociology and the process of systematization in social science research linked to class issues. She shuns a static and abstract structural-functionalist perspective of an inherent order and argues against "blaming the victim."

Much of her work points out the relationship between blocked opportunities and educational and occupational achievement. For example, in her research, she has examined reasons for the employment status gap between white and black youth despite similar skills and educational levels. She attributes anger and unrest among African American youth in this country to perpetual job discrimination and restricted access to opportunities. Hence, she notes there is a direct "causal" link between chronically unemployed black youth and racial disturbances across communities. Professor Wilkinson has also done considerable research on African-American males and their social class standing. She observes that for young people, particularly males, being employed is a mark of self-worth, strength and accomplishment. For Wilkinson, it follows then that the failure to use this resource pool in the best possible way in this nation is an extraordinary predictor of collective unrest, drug use and tensions into the adult years. She views traditionally explored predictors of family structure, teenage pregnancy, poverty and poor work habits as having failed to explain the long term problem of youth unemployment.

Using U.S. Department of Labor and Census employment data, Professor Wilkinson has carefully interpreted employer attitudes and differences in work status by race. She contends that differences in the employment position of Black and White adolescents and young adults reflect a complex set of variables that include perpetual job discrimination, restricted access to opportunities and the lack of fundamental resources. Further, she sees the preferences and predispositions of personnel staff, career placement officers, employers and managers as playing a significant role in blocking young African Americans from participating in the work world. Wilkinson describes her explanation as a rational one that reflects the realities of a race-conscious society. She points out that to the extent that African American youth are repeatedly rejected for jobs, they become frustrated and hesitant to even submit a job application. This outcome, she characterizes as resulting in a "vast pool of wasted human resources" when the door of opportunity has been closed to a youthful population (*Kentucky Kernel*, 1994).

Always providing a scholarly bent on major critical issues and social problems, Wilkinson eloquently articulates a perspective that commands attention, irrespective of whether one subscribes to her view. More importantly, however, her views are not simply idle pontificating. She seldom takes a stand on an issue without substantial research or without offering accessible solutions. For example, when racial harassment at all levels seemed to be running amuck across predominantly white campuses including that of the University of Kentucky, Wilkinson developed guidelines that document examples of racial harassment, detail employee behavior and provide a prescription for treatment. She is acutely aware of the dangers of racial harassment as well as its prevalence, which extends far beyond college-campuses. This account is similar to that of the other women sociologists from earlier and later chapters.

Based on her experiences and conversations with students, staff, and faculty across the country, she has found that racial harassment is far more "extensive, frequent, insidious and often more subtle than many other forms of harassment" (*Community Voice Newsjournal*, 1996). This specific reference to her own experience notes the importance of experiential base and access to the experiential base of others. The mission of actively fighting harassment is one that persons tend to avoid, particularly those who perceive it as someone else's problem. There are also those who recognize harassment as problematic for all persons, however, decline to fight because they do not wish to make the time investment or because the perceive it to be politically unwise. Professor Wilkinson is as steadfast in her activism as she is in her scholarship.

The commitment to combat harassment is one measurement of her combined role of scholar/activist. She rose to the occasion in a significant way when others knew something should be done, but waited for someone else to do it. While so many are aware of the irreparable damage racial harassment does to a person and to an organization, Wilkinson's "blueprint for employers" (the nickname for a recommended UK policy)emanates from acting on this awareness as well as her own experiences. The guidelines include suggestions that may be used by universities, colleges, corporations, factories, and other large and small-scale employers. In 1990, she became the first African American woman to be elected to the Vice Presidency in the 85 year history of the ASA (Blackwell, 1992: 14; Sewell, 1992: 61). Doubtless, Wilkinson, a Distinguished Professor of Arts and Sciences will continue to raise relevant questions and provide meaningful strategies for addressing social ills. What new paths will she pursue? How will she reach even broader audiences? And, what broader impact might her work have as she continues to address social change in and out the academy? (Wilkinson, 1989).

Whatever the responses to these questions, Wilkinson's contributions to issues of race meanings, gender and ethnicity embrace a "doing of sociology" unlike that of most others writing in the areas. She lends a clarity and reframing of the discourse so as to enlarge the social thought on the subjects both inside and outside the Academy, as only a politically engaged, creative intellectual would do. Crucial to this scholar's "doing sociology" is the demonstration of how one expands the parameters of knowledge by drawing upon critical substance of numerous fields. In so doing, she has been able to fashion a new and more viable way of framing the lived experience of a group whose essence still has to be captured so that transformation to a different and better world might emerge. She has integrated micro and macro theory and precis grounded in social work, social psychology, environmental sociology, culture, education, families, male-female relationships to demonstrate the need for many pieces to complete a puzzle.

Chapter Five

Delores P. Aldridge "The Wisdom of the Humanist Whole"

by Lauren Rauscher

Aims to develop theory that is emancipatory and contemplative . . . empowers women and men to actualize humanist vision of community.

—Delores P. Aldridge

Delores P. Aldridge was born in Tampa, Florida during the segregation era. Both parents were products of the public school system of Tampa and pursued technical training after high school. They parented four children, three girls and one boy with Delores being the eldest child. Though living in a racially segregated South, their home which was owned when she was two years of age was located in an area of Tampa known as Ybor City, largely populated by Latinos.

Of the six women sociologists here discussed, Aldridge is the one seen as most actively involved in three different disciplines–sociology, African American Studies, and health services/social work. The Grace Town Hamilton Distinguished Professor of Sociology and African American Studies at Emory University, she is well versed and published in each of the three disciplines and has received some of the top honors given by each. To date, the Phi Beta Kappa scholar has more than 100 awards and certificates. An international scholar who has given over 2,000 speeches in this country and abroad, Aldridge has appeared on numerous radio and television shows with editorials in major news media. She characterizes herself as a scholar activist and public intellectual dating back to her days as a participant in the Modern Civil Rights Movement of the 1960s when she was a student at Clark College in Atlanta, Georgia and later as a graduate student in the School of Social Work at Atlanta University from which she graduated as the 1,000th graduate in 1966. In 1971, she received the Ph.D. from Purdue University in Sociology. She is clear as to her identity with no struggle between the roles of scholar and activist.

Delores P. Aldridge's use of sociology, African American Studies, and social work as tools for social action for Black people reflects the advocacy cultivated in her early development as an activist in the Civil Rights Movement. Maulana Karenga acknowledges the contribution of Aldridge to womanist theory in his book *Introduction to Afro-American Studies* (1993). He uses her work to compare the difference between Black feminism and Black womanism. The latter theory, disseminated, he maintains by authors such as Rose and Aldridge, is more male inclusive and collectivistic with respect to Black people as a whole–not as a gender fragmented society.

Her invaluable work for social justice across social, demographic, and economic lines characterizes this strand of Black womanist thought as she "aims to develop theory that is emancipatory and contemplative (Aldridge, 1999, p.32) . . . [and one which] empowers women and men to actualize humanist vision of community" (p., 39). The humanist vision in the philosophical sense is immense and the steps to meeting this vision require tremendous efforts. Aldridge, like the other women in the volume, has steadfastly approached the goal from many angles; she recounts that "my hand has always been in many pots." Indeed this is the case when reviewing her extensive list of research projects and publications toward equality and social justice. Her research interests are broad, covering topics such as African American studies, facets of stratification and intergroup relations, the family, and women's health. Having interests across such a wide spectrum captures Aldridge's commitment making it difficult to pinpoint her research program and convey the depth and breadth of her important work. While her major contributions to the field of sociology appear on face to be in the areas of gender and health, Black male-female relations, gender and the labor market, and race and education, her work in African American Studies and public policy are inter-related and demonstrative of the work of an engaged social scientist.

GENDER AND HEALTH

Co-edited with LaFrancis Rodgers-Rose, Aldridge's anthology, *River of Tears: The Politics of Black Women's Health*, highlights one facet of her concern with social change at the individual and cultural levels. The focus in this work is on Black women's health. Aldridge's concern with this issue dates back to her early work as Chief of Social Services at the first Comprehensive Mental Health Program in a general hospital in the USA located in Winter Haven, Florida. This appointment was at the outset of the mental health movement in the late sixties. Her embracement of this issue is also directly related to her work as Associate Director of the Program in Women's Health Service Research, School of Medicine, Center for Clinical Evaluation Services at Emory University as well as her efforts as Chair of the Board of the International Black Women's Congress. *River of Tears* emerged from presentations and conversations at that organization's fifth national conference in 1989.

The work recognizes the need to reach out to a broad audience of women who represent academics and non-academics of different generation, which is a theme in the work and lives of other women in the book. This social engagement is summarized in the introduction to the volume, *River of Tears*, which states that it is: a collection of much needed data and available resources on Black women's health by Black women. As a result of this wide array of stories, data and resources, our daughters will be in a better position to understand and alleviate some of the politics surrounding their health, making way for another generation of Black women whose tears will be of joy and the triumph of justice in a structurally unjust society (1993:10). Aldridge's chapter in *River of Tears* explains that critical to the understanding of substantive areas of health and health care is the realization that a particular issue often transcends several areas and that occurs for numerous reasons. One such reason is to illuminate ideas about the various ways in which areas can be combined, which fits squarely into Aldridge's integrative approach to doing sociology. Another is that the distinctions among topics are fluid. There is considerable overlap and this facilitates making connections among them.

These interrelationships of various areas may underscore the wholistic way in which womanists view health and all of life. Certainly, womanists with an African centered perspective do not make the rigid distinctions made in non-African centered, male medicine between mind and body, for to do so would be to distort reality and to go against the grain of her integrative approach. For example, a discussion of sterilization of women could be done under the topic of "Reproductive Health" but it could also be just as appropriately included within the context of a discussion of "Mental Health". This would take into consideration the effect of reproduction on both the mental and physical state of the body. Similarly, in a discussion of violence against African American women, the devastating emotional effects could be considered along with the physical effects.

Aldridge argues that the greatest need in discussions of health issues facing women of African descent is to emphasize the impact of sexism, racism, and class upon them. What one generally obtains in most social science literature is a focus on the impact of one or two of these social forces without an interplay of them analyzed together. What follows is a breakdown of areas perceived as crucial for conceptualizing health of women of African descent primarily in the United States but, with some emphasis for the global community of such women (p. 17). Aldridge's approach demonstrates the importance for a field to have forces that work toward integration, which makes for a greater realization of a humane existence.

BLACK MALE-FEMALE RELATIONSHIP

Despite the large volume of scholarship on Black men and increasingly the work done about, for, and by Black women since the 1960s, Aldridge discovered a dearth of social-psychological literature on Black women's and men's relationships with one another. To begin filling this gap, she compiled *Black Male-Female Relationships: A Resource Book of Selected Materials* (1989). This volume presents selections by Black scholars on demographic, social, economic, religious and psycho-social issues related to the Black male-female dyad. "What unites all of the writings is the theme of Black male-female relationships developing and surviving in the face of tremendous odds" (p, 5). This work parallels the work on adaptation and resilience set forth earlier by Ladner and Rodgers-Rose.

Two years later, Aldridge authored *Focusing: Institutional and Interpersonal Perspectives on Black Male-Female Relations* (1991). In this book, she constructs a meta-theoretical framework, labeled the "lens theory," for understanding the heterosexual Black male-female dyad. She highlights the institutional context in which such relationships are shrouded over the life course to encourage reflection by researchers, policy makers, those in the helping professions as well as the general public. Based on a review and analysis of social science scholarship in the area of Black male-female relations since the mid 1970s, Aldridge argues for the necessity of linking interpersonal and institutional factors to understand the relationships between Black women and men. She writes, "societal problems are the reflections of ideologies and institutionalized practices" (p, 16). She asserts that the scarcity of Black men, gender role socialization, and interpersonal characteristics combine with institutional arrangements to influence the interactions between Black women and men. More specifically, Aldridge suggests that capitalism, racism, sexism, and the Judeo-Christian ethic comprise an overarching institutionalized oppressive ideology. The historical relationship of Black people to these ideologies are key to understanding how they differentially impact male-female relationships. "These four ideological institutions . . . are interlinked and form a power pattern of socialization that results in self and other oppression by Black people upon themselves and each other" (p, 26). She calls for empirical research to test her theory, specifically testing the relationship between institutions and dyadic behavior.

Recently, Aldridge and Hemmons (2001) apply the theoretical *Lens Model* to Black male-female violence. They focus attention to how major structural factors—capitalism, racism, sexism, and the Judeo-Christian ethic—operate in tandem to affect violence between Black men and Black women (see figure 5.1). The approach used in the work was based on the case study method-

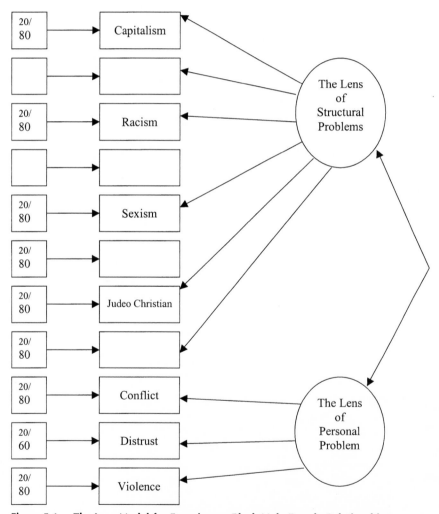

Figure 5.1.   The Lens Model for Focusing on Black Male Female Relationship

ology. Again they conclude with an appeal for further research to disaggregate out the nuances, intricacies, and mechanisms through which these complex structural systems, such as the economy and religion, operate.

GENDER AND THE LABOR MARKET

Aldridge's research on Black women in the labor market spans 30 years. Her work reviews broad historical trends, emphasizes the importance of theoretical understanding, and provides prescriptions for social policy. Her interest in this area began as she questioned just how far Black women had "made it" as the media and others bombarded them with "you've come a long way baby" (Aldridge, 1975). Analyses since the mid-1970s illustrate that although there have been gains, Black women have still not attained their fullest potential. Black women continue to be disadvantaged in the U.S. economy.

Moreover, Aldridge has demonstrated that historically Black women have worked in the paid labor force at higher rates than other groups of women. She argues that this rate of higher participation is in large part due to the necessity to economically support themselves and their families. She also indicates that the increased rate of production during World War II, Civil Rights legislation for fair employment policies, and increased educational advancements are factors that have affected Black women's work. She uses Census data to track the occupational shifts of Black women over time, from the 1910s to 1980s. While her work predates Wilkinson, there is similarity for both trace these Black women's work from agriculture to domestic work followed by an increase in semi-skilled manufacturing during World War II. The 1960s and 1970s witnessed an increase in their labor force participation overall and in the (semi) professions as some of the legal barriers that African American women had faced were lifted. Despite such changes, Aldridge shows that Black women continue to struggle in the economic market place. She dispels the myths that Black women are the recipients of double benefits due to being Black and female, highlighting that they are disproportionately concentrated in low-wage service jobs and have the lowest earnings of any race/sex group (Aldridge 1989). She calls for collective action—possibly with white women and/or with Black men—to "change the system so that it ceases to be racist, chauvinistic, or rooted in inequities" (Aldridge 1989: 151).

Most recently, Aldridge (1999) looks ahead to the employment prospects and barriers that Black women face in the 21st century. The Information Age is dominated by science and high technology. However, despite gains in educational attainment, she reveals that African American women are not found in high-tech occupations such as sophisticated information technology, the natural sciences, and engineering. This work complements scholarship that illustrates the scarcity of women and men of color and White women with college degrees in the natural sciences technology and engineering. The findings suggest recommendations, for without such there is a gap in the reality and the possibilities for change.

In analyzing many current descriptions of the occupational status of Black women, Aldridge asserts,

> To provide statistics that focus upon participation or lack of participation in the job market without also providing explanations of and actions for altering inequity is of little value for ensuring black women's survival and full engagement in the labor market of the twenty first century (Aldridge 1999: 376).

Thus, she concludes with a proposal for a model with African centered underpinnings designed to "understand and promote the engagement of Black women in the new world order" with the purpose to transform institutions and values (Aldridge, 1999: 370). The model is labeled "HEAL" which stands for *Historical-Cultural Experiences, Equity and Action for the Labor Market.*

Aldridge argues that it is critical to place Black women's labor market experiences within historical and cultural context while addressing educational and employment equity. She also feels that the model is useful when implementing action-oriented strategies to transform institutions and values. She provides a list of broad intervention strategies to bring attention to Black women's place in the Information Age and increase access, recruitment, and retention of Black women in high tech occupations such as microelectronic specialists, genomic data analysts, computer disc designers, etc.

RACE, EDUCATION AND AFRICAN AMERICAN STUDIES

Aldridge began her productive academic career with her first published research in the areas of gender and family studies (1977) and race and education (1978) and has continued to study these areas while delving into others. In her first published work on race and education, she focused on "Litigation and Education of Blacks: Another Look at the U.S. Supreme Court," where she skillfully traced and analyzed the Court's role in the segregation/desegregation struggle of African Americans in education. She contends that the Supreme Court has played a very crucial role in dealing with race and educational issues throughout the years, as evidenced in the historic *Plessy v. Ferguson (1896) decision*, the *Brown v. Board of Education decision (1954)*, and the *Swann v. Charlotte-Mecklenburg Board of Education decision (1971)*. Moreover, Aldridge (1975) provides an historical review of the US Supreme Court's role in the racial segregation-desegregation struggle from 1877–1970s. She employs a macro (institutional) framework looking specifically to the role of the courts in (re)acting to issues of equal access to equal facilities and educational experiences for Blacks.

Aldridge (1975) argues that "courts were the most consistent protectors of the rights of Black students," yet there was a tremendous "failure of Congress" and "failure of the executive department" under five presidents to implement the mandates handed down through the judicial system. Thus, it was 1970 and the Southern states were still slow to change their educational policies and practices towards African Americans. Further, she reasons that the desegregation of the nation's public educational institutions has been an emotional partisan process. In this process, both the educational institutions and the Court have made sweeping promises which were tied to reality by neither research nor insight. At the time of her critique of the role of the Supreme Court in 1978, she concluded that the school desegregation appeared to stalemate as the courts gradually retreated from their position of the fifties and sixties. Moving from a critical analysis in this work, throughout the 1980s and 1990s she continued to focus on race and educational issues with respect to diversity and cultural democracy.

In 1994, she writes a scorching editorial in the *Chicago Tribune* (February 21, Section 1) that crystallizes her views on African American Studies and multiculturalism. This editorial emerged from a monograph (1994) on the subject and subsequently was an editorial in the *Emory Multicultural Newsletter*. The substance of the editorial and other articles on the subject can, perhaps, best be captured by the following excerpt:

> Black studies was treated with disdain and contempt with both individual and institutional resistance to the pioneers of the field. As such much energy and time was expended in intergroup conflict of personalities and ideas–energies that could have been channeled into more creative scholarship, program development and campus vitality. So much time was spent on the question of "whether rather than "whither." That is the focus of many of the administrators and faculty were caught up in whether the field was relevant for the academy rather than how to meaningfully incorporate it so that the university would begin to deal with the "universe" as it purported to do.

Aldridge goes on to write:

> A renewed emphasis on race is in order. American universities and the society need to look inward to face the racial challenge. They need to find ways that allow all groups to give of their best and work to eliminate the worst of their

attributes to make this a society of anticipatory democracy for all. Anglo Saxons are neither better nor worse than any other group in the university or the society, but they have been the dominant group. There is now a new challenge to this dominance with the increasing numerical presence of diverse groups.

The activist posture of Aldridge is a trademark no matter what the forum. As a dedicated teacher at Emory University, she has nurtured the development of cross disciplinary and cross cultural directions. She has consistently advocated that intellectual discourse has limitless possibilities not to be geographically or culturally limited but reflective of the universe. The *Emory Magazine* in 1989 dubbed Aldridge as one of the individuals who had made a difference in the institution's development. *Emory Intellectual Initiatives*, January 2001, in describing a half dozen of its scholars who are considered visionaries, stated "Decades ago, sociologist Delores Aldridge recognized the cultural necessity of a scholarly understanding of the experience of African Americans. Such creative and determined professors defy the tweedy stereotypes of academics and define a new class of intellectual entrepreneurs." None of these accolades came easily for her when in 1971 she became the first African American woman faculty in the university and Founding Director of Black Studies (later African American and African Studies) at an institution in the deep south, unaccustomed to African Americans or white women as professors or administrators.

This institution had only admitted its first African American student in 1962 and white women six years prior to the admission of the first African American male. Serving as an administrator for two decades in Black Studies was a monumental accomplishment, for freshly minted doctorates traditionally ground themselves in their research at major research institutions. They do not enter into the academy as administrators. And, freshly minted doctorates certainly do not tread in untested waters of pioneering a new field. Further, it is an anomaly for such an individual to stay grounded with pioneering a field for so long while developing and maintaining a presence in the discipline in which she was trained. But, Aldridge is "doing sociology" by demonstrating how it could be used in innovative ways that was to have lasting impact on higher education.

No less crucial to her advocacy posture was the editing of special issues of prominent journals: *The Journal of Black Studies (1989)* and *Phylon: A Review of Race and Culture (1992)*, a journal founded at Atlanta University by W. E. B. DuBois. The special issues focused on Black Women and Black Studies in the Academy. In them, questions were raised and suggestions were provided for strategies to improve the status of Black women in the United States and the role and place of Black Studies in the curriculum. She had earlier (1979) written about the challenge of interfacing American and Afro-American Studies in which she articulated the rationale for a distinct discipline of Afro-American Studies. In doing so, she emphasized that no other field had placed African Americans at the center of the discourse nor could or should these longer existing disciplines have done so since African Americans relationship to themselves and the world was not the reason for the other disciplines coming into existence. Her volume, *Out of the Revolution: The Development of Africana Studies (2000)*, co-edited with Carlene Young is based on original research unparalleled by any other work on the subject to date. One of her own chapters, based on surveying 1600 institutions, gives the most up-to-date analysis of the present status of the discipline in institutions of American higher education which parallels work done by Jackson when she provided data on Black female sociologists.

More recently Daudi Azibo (2001), writing on Black Studies, states "Aldridge's visionary model that extends Black Studies beyond the U.S. Diaspora which was posited in 1984 is one which the discipline would do well to focus upon. In charting new directions for Black Studies, she was "doing sociology" by critiquing the racial equity framework for disseminating knowledge in higher education. Note equity is used in this chapter. However, the terms equity, equality, and liberty appear throughout the work and are used with similar meanings by each of the women sociologists.

SOCIOLOGY AND PUBLIC POLICY

While breaking barriers and challenging tradition had become a trademark of Aldridge, as though the challenges at Emory were not enough, earlier in 1980–81, accepted an Intergovernment Personnel Act Appointment with the USDA Forest Service in Washington, D.C. In doing so, she became the first sociologist to be employed by the Forest Service as a policy analyst. Also, in only one year, she amassed considerable work in environmental sociology and public policy. She authored eight pieces of work in less than one full calendar year. These included a monograph, *Overcoming Conflict: the Public Agency Responds (1983) and The Use of Pesticides—A Social Issue (1981)*. These were major pieces of work which became the guides for the Forest Service dealing with public constituents and USDA Forest Service practices throughout its 22,000 labor force. What Aldridge offered were explanations for the origin of the problems drawing upon sociological and social work theoretical knowledge and practices of dealing with people. This was particularly relevant for the Forest Service in dealing with a public which in reality is the owner of government lands.

After careful analysis of the problems, she presents strategies for addressing them. The sharing of her scholarship and developmental skills serving as a policy analyst with the Forest Service proved invaluable. She authored the *Social Impact Assessment Policy Guidelines,* which were published in the *Federal Register* less than nine months after her assignment to the project, a feat not easily accomplished in the U.S. Federal government.

At the present, Aldridge continues to write on issues in African American Studies, gender, race and education, and male female relationships as she plans new and exciting projects already underway. She has been asked on numerous occasions if she will move into the upper echelons of administration in a university. Aldridge maintains, however, that at this time such positions do not hold the appeal that continuing policy-relevant research and teaching do. Why is she not interested in a deanship/presidency? It may be because she has tired of administration having served for two decades as an administrator of an Africana Studies Program as well as President of four national organizations, administered major projects and served on over 2000 committees including fund raisers for a variety of charity events. She also has more interest in the international arena, particularly in Africa where she is involved in numerous development projects including establishing a health clinic, a community center, and educational training fund to provide college scholarships and technology to colleges. Based on three decades of extraordinary accomplishments as a scholar-activist and public intellectual, Aldridge's future projects will certainly address social justice with continued rigor and excellence.

Crucial to this scholar's "doing" is the demonstrations of how one expands the parameters of knowledge by drawing upon critical substance of numerous fields, and, in doing so, is able to fashion a new and more viable way of framing the lived experiences of a group whose essence still has to be captured so that transformation to a different and better world might emerge. She has integrated micro and macro theory and precis grounded in social work, social psychology, environmental sociology, culture, education, families, and male-female relationships all of which demonstrate the need for many pieces to complete a puzzle.

Chapter Six

Vivian V. Gordon "Self Defining as Fundamental"

A people's definition of self and role is the most fundamental statement of their social reality

—Vivian V. Gordon

This chapter highlights one of those black female sociologists, Vivian Verdell Gordon, who was an exemplary individual. She overcame many obstacles to become a prolific sociologist, both academic and applied, and was a relentless activist, and poet. Unfortunately, her death in March 1995, after a struggle with muscle degeneration, left many of her projects incomplete. Nonetheless, her specific perspectives and ideologies clearly emerge from her research and work. Vivian V. Gordon was born in Washington, DC and with the exception of a short period of time in Los Angeles, spent most of her life on the east coast. She received a BS in physics and social science in 1955 from Virginia State University and an M.A. in sociology from the University of Pennsylvania. While she was completing her master's degree, she was employed as a social worker for the child welfare division of the women's Christian Alliance Child Welfare Agency.

In 1977, two years after receiving her B.S., Vivian Gordon completed her M.A. At this point, she decided not to pursue a Ph.D., but continued to be actively involved in numerous projects. Her interest in education is reflected in the types of projects in which she chose to involve herself. From 1957 to 1963, Gordon was an education and social science analyst for the Education and Public Welfare Division of the Congressional Reference Service, coordinator of research for a special study of the House Committee on Education and Labor, and a research assistant for the Congressional Reference Service—Library of Congress.

In 1966, Gordon's interest in youth and education took her to Los Angeles where she was the organizer and associate director of the Upward Bound Project of the University of California-Los Angeles until 1967. Subsequently, she remained in Los Angeles as the director of the Educational Participation in Communities Program at California State College. During her tenure in California, Gordon made the decision to return to the east coast to pursue a Ph.D. in sociology, which she received in 1974 from the University of Virginia, Charlottesville.

It is difficult to pinpoint precisely when Gordon developed interest in her many areas of specialization. Over the course of her career, she cultivated specialties in African American Studies, race/ethnic and gender relations, social psychology, and women's studies as it relates to Africana womanism. Many of these areas blended together in her research. She was particularly interested in continuity and change in the Black community, African American social movements, the dynamics of racism and prejudice, and collective behavior. Upon returning to study for her Ph.D., Gordon focused her research on "those matters which had demanded her attention during her prior extensive work experience" (Gordon 1985, p.65). She directed her attention to contributing new models and paradigms for explanation of the African-American experience. Her dissertation, *The Self-Concept of Black Americans*, was the result of her interest in Black youth's self-perceptions with regards to the negation of the importance of culture for those young people (Gordon 1985).

In 1974, Dr. Gordon completed her Ph.D. and remained at the University of Virginia as an assistant professor in the department of sociology and director for the program in African American Studies. In 1979, she was promoted to associate professor in the department of sociology and relinquished her position as director for the program in African American Studies. During this period of time, Gordon published four books, which included her dissertation. These books included a selected bibliography of publications with major emphasis on education, a collection of essays written by black scholars on black issues, and topics such as integration in public education programs. She also published eight articles in various scholarly journals on a variety of topics that encompassed her major areas of interest, such as the Black community, the self-concept of Black Americans, education, and African-American studies programs.

In 1985, Vivian Gordon left the sociology department at the University of Virginia to chair the African and Afro-American Studies Department at the State University of New York at Albany where she had a tumultuous situation subsequently leaving the position due to her deteriorating health and the struggles with faculty and administration over the development and direction of the field of Africana Studies. With the exception of one year from 1986–1987 when she was a visiting scholar at Wellesley College in Massachusetts, she remained at SUNY-Albany until her death. She was as prolific during these years as in her prior years at Virginia. Gordon published six books on topics such as the viability of coalitions between black and white women, African-American family patterns, and understanding prisons and the justice system for youth. She also published five articles on similar topics. In addition, she produced a series of educational television and special teaching tapes, conducted several professional workshops and training sessions, and published a book of poetry entitled *For Dark Women and Others* under the name Satiafa.

Throughout her academic career she was a popular public intellectual on the speaking circuit. She frequently appeared as a guest speaker in extended lecture presentations. She was featured on more than nine radio and television shows, including *ABC News Nightwatch* and *C-SPAN*. Furthermore, she was cited in presses such as *The New York Times, USA Today*, and *ABC News*. Although she appeared on many popular television and radio shows, as well as special news features, she did not limit herself to these media. Gordon frequently appeared in community-based programs and received numerous honors and awards for her community service. Gordon was also heavily involved with her students and in campus activities at each institution where she taught. In addition to workshops and teaching tapes, she was popular with her students as a professor and received a number of teaching honors and awards. Beyond teaching and the walls of academia, she was involved in numerous off-campus student programs, primarily during her years at SUNY-Albany.

Professionally, Gordon was strong in her position of limiting her associations primarily to African-American organizations, as she maintained most white scholars limit their affiliations to predominantly white organizations. Unlike Aldridge, who led and participated in both predominately white and predominately black organizations and, Wilkinson who led and participated in predominately white organizations, Gordon chose to participate in predominately Black organizations and publish with Black presses. Notably, she served on the executive boards of both Blacks in Government and the National Council for Black Studies, where she was instrumental in the development of the Black Studies Curriculum Guidelines. She also sat on the editorial boards of the *Journal of Black Studies* from 1984 to 1989, the *Negro Educational Review* from 1980 to 1983 and *The Black Books Bulletin* throughout the decade of the 1980s. Throughout her career, Vivian Verdelle Gordon remained active as a scholar, applied sociologist, activist, community leader, and poet. With ten published books, thirteen articles, numerous presentations, and several sponsored research projects, Gordon was well established as a writer, speaker, and researcher. At the time of her death in March 1995, she left many unfinished works in progress.

Completing her master's work before or at the very beginning of the Civil Rights Movement in combination with many other barriers, Gordon is one of those strong, outstanding individuals that made it in spite of the obstacles placed before her. Why her work, like other pioneering Black women sociologists, has not been more widely recognized, remains to be explained. Potential explanations tend to intertwine into a "web" of factors. One reasonable conclusion may be that the interaction of both her race and gender create an invisibility as previously discussed. While some of the invisibility of Vivian V. Gordon, and other women like her, may be directly attributable to this phenomenon, it may also be the case that social identity exerts an indirect effect through the areas of interest that these individuals pursue and the type of research they conduct. Mainstream sociology tends to be more accepting of certain types of research and certain areas at various times. Consequently, the type of research a scholar is conducting may also add to their relative exclusion form real recognition in academia. Often, it appears to occur in cycle, where both the research on and by a subordinate group is virtually invisible. Because many individual members of that group are studying aspects of that and other excluded groups, they are at an even greater disadvantage.

As previously discussed, Gordon's work tended to involve research about African Americans and women. And, while research on and by each of these groups has gained visibility, it has not reached the levels as that of the majority group in sociology. Because it is this literature that has remained fairly unrecognized in sociology, as well as African-American Studies, attention will be focused upon exploring some of the works of Vivian V. Gordon in the areas of Black women, feminism, Black liberation, and Black studies (Gordon 1991; Johnson 1975).

GORDON'S WORKS AND IDEAS

Gordon's work involved a variety of topics and issues over the course of her career. The central focus remained on black Americans with special emphasis on youth and women. A number of her works consist of edited volumes, results of applied research and compiled bibliographies on specific topics. Much of her work was conveyed through her teaching, public presentations, and community activity. Possibly as another consequence of a group's marginalization in a discipline, some of what does exist in certain journals is not widely disseminated. Consequently, the tendency is to look to a few pivotal works to capture some important aspects of Gordon's contributions, perspectives, and research. The limited dissemination of some publications may become less relevant with the Internet–it is much easier to locate articles on a topic. So, perhaps, the pertinent question will be not so much the physical dissemination of written work but the extent to which we choose to teach it.

THE SELF-CONCEPT OF BLACK AMERICANS

The most appropriate place to begin in Dr. Gordon's work on Black women is with the topic of her dissertation in which she explores the self-concept of Black Americans. Although this research does not focus specifically on women, it is her first significant academic work that aptly applies to both African-American women, as well as men. In this volume, she challenges the popularly held belief that Black Americans have low self-concepts. Gordon (1980, Introduction) addresses three questions in this regard, (1) What has been the historical background of Black self-concept research? (2) What are some of the methodological problems with the research? And, (3) What are some directions in the theoretical orientation of the research?

Gordon surveys the studies that have measured the self-concepts of African-Americans. As a trained social psychologist, she begins with the theories and research of George Herbert Mead and Charles Horton Cooley. Through the numerous surveys considered, she argues that at least two problems emerge in these studies (Gordon, 1980). First, they all presume Black self-derogation as a result of slavery and oppression in the United States. Second, they all contain fundamental measurement problems. She further argues that the previous studies have a problem with defining self-concept and problems with validity. That is, there is no consistent definition that occurs in the self-concept literature. The definitions vary from uni-dimensional concepts, focusing on a single component, to multi-dimensional concepts, considering a variety of components to the self. In addition, the instruments of measurement, including scales and dimensions, vary and frequently fail to measure the true essence of the self-concept.

Gordon concludes that the evidence cited in support of the contention that Black Americans have negative self-concepts is inconsistent and inconclusive. Generalized statements about low Black self-concepts are largely a function of (1) the research instrument that was used, (2) the theoretical orientation of the researcher, and (3) the time and place of the study (Gordon, 1981). Based on these conditions, the findings of the studies produced enough variation to warrant careful reconsideration of the definition of self-concept and the instruments used to measure it. Gordon's contributions extend beyond a discussion of African-Americans to an important contribution to the field of social psychology. She contrasts the previous definitions of self-concept in terms of their complexity and contextualization. She contends that multi-dimensional definitions far better capture an individual's self-concept. That is, an individual possesses a multiplicity of self-concepts for his or her various identities. For example, an individual may have a higher self-concept as a student than as an athlete. In addition, some of the studies she examines argue for the existence of a global self-concept. According to these theorists, individuals carry around a typical, or average, self-concept that is the mean of their individual self-concept scores for their various identities. This global self-concept is carried through every situation the individual encounters. Again, she argues against the existence of such a concept. Instead, she suggests that self-concepts are not only multi-dimensional, but contextual. The score of a person's self-concept will vary in different situations and contexts which frequently depends on the reference group involved.

Through questioning the validity of previous studies and definitions of self-concept, she makes a particularly important contribution to the understanding of African-Americans. While, she concludes that the overall self-concept of Black Americans is not as low as previously believed, she also suggests that their self-concepts are affected by the reference group involved in a particular context. When African-Americans do compare themselves to white Americans in specific situations, their self-concepts are typically lower. The logical implication is that, overall, Black Americans tend not to use white Americans as a reference group in forming their self-concepts. With this work, Gordon critiques the previous literature on self-concepts and proposes different definitions for future research. Her work joins a small group of Black women who have focused on self-esteem and self-concept in their work (Aldridge 1971; Wilkinson 1995; Rodgers-Rose 1980; Myers 1991). Most notably, Lena Wright Myers (1991) contends that Black women "cope better" because they use themselves as a reference group, rather than White women. In spite of the fact that this piece is not widely cited, Gordon makes a significant contribution to the discipline of social psychology and African-American studies.

BLACK WOMEN: FEMINISM, BLACK LIBERATION, AND BLACK STUDIES

Gordon's work on the self-concept of Black Americans resurfaces in many of her later works and forms the crux of her conceptual frame of reference. "A people's definition of self and role is the most fundamental statement of their social reality" (Gordon, 1991, p.1). In the United States, the net result of a pattern of sanctioned, structured inequality is the systematic imposition of advantage based on skin color (Gordon, 1991). Although Black Americans do not have low self-concepts to the degree previously proposed, they do consistently experience the effects of institutionalized, non-gender specific racism. Both Black men and women have been victims of the indignities of racism in the United States.

BLACK WOMEN AND FEMINISM

Black women are accountable to issues of racism primarily and sexism secondarily. Unlike Black men and white women, they are thrice victimized by racism, sexism, and economic oppression. Consequently, they are frequently unable to distinguish the source of their oppression at any one time (Gordon 1991). Sometimes, these oppressions exert their forces simultaneously and equally (Gordon 1991) and issues of racism are inextricably linked to issues of sexism for Black women. In order to address the issues of Black women, one must not only address the needs of Black women, "but the historic primacy of African and African-American communities" (Gordon 1985, p. viii). Therefore, to consider the effects of sexism, Black women must first confront the issue of racism.

Within this conceptual framework, Gordon questions the viability of coalitions between black and white women against sexism in her volume, *Black Women: Feminism and Black Liberation: Which Way?* It is not difficult to determine that she believes it is not useful, and sometimes precarious, for Black women to join with white women on feminist issues. She considers a number of factors that illustrate her argument. The second wave of the feminist movement, which began in the 1960s, was pioneered primarily by white, middle class women. As a direct consequence, feminism became conceptually exclusive based on a gender specific identity (Gordon 1991). These women primarily felt the effects of sexism. Black women must first confront the issue of racism.

One of her most crucial arguments considers the basic tenet of traditional coalition theory. This theory "underscores the necessity for a strategic evaluation of the basic power in the reward phase of the effort as a requirement for partnership, if there would be a meaningful and nondestructive achievement for the component with the lesser power" (Gordon 1985, p.3). White women have historically and presently benefited from their linkages with white men. Based on traditional coalition theory, this indicates that coalitions with white women are a poor choice for African-American women (Gordon 1985).

To support this contention, she creates *The Gordon Schema*[1] to depict the power of relationships among African-American, European-American, and other non-white men and women. In the first diagram, she illustrates the socio-economic and political linkages between these groups. She concludes from this diagram that there are direct linkages between the men and women *within* each of these groups, but that there are only ambiguous, weak linkages *between* the various groups. Therefore, limited communication and common-alities regarding their historic and contemporary experiences and goals negate the benefits of coalitions between these groups according to Gordon.

Beyond the potential for communication, she considers the relative power of each of these groups over other groups on five dimensions: (1) economic domination, (2) political dominance, (3) cultural domination, (4) physical domination, and (5) military power. The overall argument in these models is that Black women and other non-white women have the least power of any of these groups. They do not exercise domination over any other group on any of the five dimensions. Primarily through their linkages to white men, white women possess some power over each of the other groups, with exception to white men. Because white women do exercise a race-based domination over

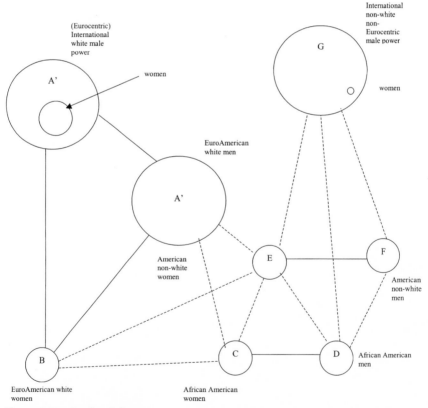

Figure 6.1.   Gordon Schema

African-American women, a coalition between these two groups would violate the tenet of traditional coalition theory. Gordon suggests that the more viable coalition would occur between other non-white American women and African-American women. Although, these coalitions may also present issues of concern based on the limited communication, resulting in a lack of shared understandings, experiences, and goals between the two groups.

Gordon's overall conclusion in this volume is that the nature of oppression experienced by black and white women is significantly different. Therefore, the goals they pursue toward the end of oppression are objectively different or partially non-overlapping. African-American women can not isolate the primacy of their racial oppression from issues of gender oppression. Joining or forming gender-specific coalitions with white women does not address the centrality of oppression for African American women. Instead, they:

> Must contribute to the development of theoretical perspectives which allow for movement away from the locked-in application of models and paradigms developed for a Eurocentric society to Afrocentric beliefs and lifestyles (Gordon 1985, p. ix).

BLACK WOMEN AND BLACK STUDIES

The earliest Black studies programs were established as a result of the protest movements of the late 1950s and 1960s (Gordon, 1991; Gordon, 1981). They were formed as a means of meeting the demands of the students. During this time, Black men and women joined together in pursuit of strong, academically founded Black Studies programs in higher education. As a Black woman, a professor in an African-American studies program, and a key member in the development of the first Black Studies Curriculum Guideline for the National Council for Black Studies, Gordon was particularly interested in the position of women within these programs. Her call for a shift of focus from feminism to Afrocentric perspectives as the key to ending the oppression of Black women and men especially strengthened her interest in the gender content of Black Studies programs. Consequently, she was critical of the direction that these programs were taking.

In many instances, the programs became male-centered, internalizing the traditional concept of "the academy" (Gordon, 1991). As in the women's studies programs that followed on the coattails of African-American studies, Black women were relatively under-represented in both content and in administrative positions. Although some Black women found support from Black males, there was an unanticipated sexism exhibited by Black males

(Gordon, 1991). In light of the importance Gordon places on the strength of the African American community over feminism toward the end of oppression, this phenomenon is and continues to be vital. Steps must be taken within African-American Studies programs to recognize the presence and contributions of the women in the field. Perhaps, the most cited work dealing with this issue was that written by Aldridge (1992).

Vivian V. Gordon was a female sociologist who made significant contributions to individuals, groups, the discipline of sociology, and African-American Studies. She did not limit herself to one method of disseminating her knowledge and work, but channeled herself through a variety of media. She left virtually no means of communication unused. As a result, she left a marked impact, in spite of the obstacles she faced. Though we may only hypothesize as to the reasons why her work is not widely known in mainstream sociology, it was not for a lack of production on her part. Her work on the self-concept of Black Americans challenged the belief that African-Americans have low self-concepts as well as provided theoretical contributions particularly the situational activation orientation. Furthermore, she made notable suggestions for the measurement of self-concepts for future research. Her work on Black women specifically provides careful critiques of the directions they, as Black and as women, should pursue toward the elimination of oppression.

The purpose of this essay is to provide some insight into the life and work of Vivian Verdell Gordon with focus on selected works. This essay serves as a beginning point for a deeper analysis of the breadth and substance of her work that may be pursued in future research. In addition, while this essay only explores the life and work of one notable Black female sociologist, it serves as a contribution to this volume which seeks to highlight research on and by black women in sociology.

NOTE

1. Though these schema are conceptually useful, they are problematic in terms of methodology and operationalization. Gordon creates these diagrams without documentation of a source of data or evidence to support her classifications. In addition, she does not fully operationalize her concepts, providing clear definitions of what she is attempting to measure. Finally, she does not fully document her method of classification. That is, how she determined the assignment of particular values to particular groups.

Chapter Seven

Common Intellectual Threads of Those Who Dare "Imagine . . . "

Jacquelyne Johnson Jackson, LaFrancis Rodgers-Rose, Joyce A. Ladner, Doris Wilkinson, Delores P. Aldridge and Vivian V. Gordon all approach sociology from a politically-engaged stance. They pay attention to the world outside of academia and recommend practical solutions to the problems that they feel are most pressing. Further, all six scholars use sociology to disprove dominant myths about Black women, are concerned with the survival of African Americans as a whole, and work both inside and outside of the Academy. But, perhaps, more important, each of these scholars gives insights into the caliber of their minds and the force of their personalities in impacting social change. They all "do sociology" in their own unique way.

Each of these women approaches her work from a different perspective on social change and each of their perspectives coincides with the times. These scholars' research and recommendations offer a wealth of knowledge for academics and non-academics alike. In order to fully understand their contributions, there is need for more information about their lives and work. What led them to sociology? Where did their commitment to a politically-engaged approach originate and how does it connect with their personal histories and day-to-day lives? What advice do they have for other sociologists seeking to conduct socially relevant research and to facilitate positive social change?

African American women comprise fewer than 1.9% of all academic sociologists in the United States (Kulis and Miller in Brewer, 1989:65). As the above discussions of the work of six of these scholars suggest, however, their proportional contributions to the field and to policy have been, and continue to be, enormous. Jacquelyn J. Jackson opens new vistas for understanding and advocating positive change for the aged. She "does sociology" for the aged that provides directives for all interested in gerontology. Her intellectual grasp and her tremendous energy in rethinking and recasting ways of working with the aging sets forth some of the most useful models to which we have access.

LaFrancis Rodgers-Rose "does sociology" unlike any other scholar, as she "brings to life" the challenges to and the promises of the experiences of Black women's lives. She is ever true to her "African center" incorporating it as she "does sociology" in all of her scholarship and precis. The organization which she created, The International Black Women's Congress, is a testimony of "putting into practice what you preach."

Joyce A. Ladner gave the world one of the most meaningful empirical works on the lives of young Black women of limited financial means. For her "doing sociology" required her to take off the objective dispassionate lens and remember that "she was on many levels one of them/her subjects." In "doing sociology," she had to address the racism of the field and point out its failure to realize its promise with the race factor at the helm of her motivation. Moreover, both at the micro and macro levels, Ladner breathes new life into "old" social science.

Doris Wilkinson "does sociology" by bringing new meaning to so many old ways of viewing critical concepts. She traverses so many of the sub areas of sociology yielding new insights, useful inside and outside of the academy. She never ceases to find new ways of presenting the lives of Black people in a realistic way. Her work on the rethinking of and different applications for the concept "minority" is potentially revolutionary.

Delores P. Aldridge, exemplifying the wisdom of the humanist whole, ever the scholar activist in and outside of the academy in a seemingly seamless fashion, gives new meaning to "doing sociology." Though risking "discipline suicide" by stepping out of the box of sociology, she "does sociology" to participate in the creation of yet another discipline—Black/Africana Studies. But, her visionary work, like that of the other women sociologists in this book, spans many subareas, including the family, education, gender, and social theory with her own "*Lens Theory*" for understanding male-female relationships. But, also mindful of how the world needs the scholar to share skills in other arenas, Aldridge "does sociology" in the public sector, forging new paths with models for social policy.

Vivian V. Gordon, self-defining as fundamental, did her sociology through a variety of media outlets. In doing so, she was able to disseminate her knowledge and skills to many inside and outside of the Academy. Her work on self-concepts was a valuable contribution to research as well as her work on women which provided careful analyses of and directions for Black people, both men and women, in pursuit of the elimination of oppression. She made valuable contributions to the African American Studies and public advocacy.

The presentation of "slices" of the lives of six women sociologists suggests the need for focusing on the lives of more of these women. Life histories of Black female sociologists could fill a gaping hole in the literature on the lives and work of prominent U.S. sociologists. Combined with a full understanding of their written work, their life histories will contribute valuable theoretical and practical information about the relationship between race and gender both inside and outside of the Academy. But, their stories will do more than that. They will expand knowledge about the extraordinary scholarship of African American women beyond the areas of race and gender to a broader range of relevant subject areas. When this is done, they like other groups, can be appreciated for their exceptional skills and insights on their own group as others have always done. But unlike most other scholars, they have gone beyond "their world" to facilitate understanding of "other worlds" and the relationships of these "worlds" to each other. They have brought their lived experiences to their sociological work which have helped to explain social issues outside of their own experiential base thus shedding light on how different experiences can impact each other.

The life histories of the six Black female sociologists discussed would be particularly valuable because their lives and work illuminate a range of approaches to politically-engaged scholarship. Sociologists who approach their work from a politically-engaged stance strengthen the discipline by increasing its relevance to the world in which we live. Jacquelyne J. Jackson, LaFrancis Rodgers-Rose, Joyce A. Ladner, Doris Wilkinson, Delores P. Aldridge and Vivian V. Gordon have forged strong connections between sociology and the world outside of academia. While the sections on each scholar are useful, they do not present an in depth context necessary for a full understanding of the contributions that each scholar has made to sociology and to the larger society. Life histories could provide that context.

Further study could explore the life histories of these and other Black female sociologists with particular attention paid to the connections between sociology and social change in the subjects' lives and perceptions. Interviews could be structured around a particular set of themes and/or topics. Although the topics for initial interviews are outlined below, the data would likely yield patterns and themes to inform subsequent interviews.

An initial round of interviews could focus on the life path that led each scholar to a career as a sociologist. Questions might include (but are not limited to): (1) "When did you decide to become a sociologist?" (2) "Who in your life encouraged or discouraged you from pursuing your goal?" and (3)"Were there specific obstacles that you faced in moving toward your goal? If so, what were they?" (4) What barriers or unique problems have you encountered during the course of your career? Researchers and students might also explore the life path that led each scholar to activism outside of sociology; the development of their theories of social change; their experiences in academic departments and their experiences in non-academic work. Another topic of special interest could be their advice to aspiring politically-engaged sociologists.

In addition, politically-engaged scholarship invites attention to the researchers' social location. The term "social location" refers not only to race, gender, class and other identities, but also to the historical, ideological and economic contours in which those identities exist. A focus on power dynamics is crucial to an analysis of social location. As Ladner and others point out, many white scholars—males and females—have used their race privilege to define Black women—their histories and their identities. Particularly important in the framing of these implications is the fact that white scholars (including white feminist scholars) have too often built their careers by extracting information about Black women's lives and then documenting their views of these and theorizing about those experiences. Unfortunately, institutionalized racism and sexism within academia have created a milieu in which "Black women too often have offered the experiences while others told them what their experiences mean" (Brewer, 1989: 65).

Attention to the power dynamics of research—particularly (in this case) the power dynamics of race and gender—moves discussions of the researchers' and subjects' social locations beyond the data. White sociologists lacking the history, experience, and personal insight must be cautious if they are to adequately represent the views of Black women. White male and female researchers studying the careers of Black female sociologists would be well-advised to consider the implications of their own social locations as different from those that they study. The purpose of this work has been to enhance our understanding of the work of six politically-engaged Black female sociologists—Jacquelyne J. Jackson, LaFrancis Rodgers-Rose and Joyce A. Ladner, Doris Wilkinson, Delores P. Aldridge and Vivian V. Gordon. Their scholarship has often been minimized in the literature by and about sociologists. This minimizing or overshadowing serves only to limit a broader understanding of so many salient issues for sociologists and the U.S. society as a whole.

Chapter Eight

Summary

This work has attempted throughout to discuss six female sociologists who received terminal degrees in sociology between 1960 and 1975 and who chose to spend much of their professional lives within the Academy. While there are others who received degrees within this framework, access to relevant information and/or approval for incorporation in the volume was unsuccessful for meeting a publication deadline. Some of the women who were not included, will be the focus of a companion volume. Each of the six women included held a "common bond" of geographical and social location, as they each grew up in a segregated South. In presenting these women, the book sought to demonstrate how each contributed to what C. Wright Mills called "the sociological imagination" and how each helped the reader assess the uniqueness of a black female sociological perspective. The questions raised were as follows: 1) What is the unique perspective brought to the sociological table by pioneering black female sociologists? 2) Why this particular sociology is different? and, 3) What does this different sociological perspective mean for sociology as a discipline? A glimpse into an original work by each of the sociologists is appended for the reader's scrutiny.

All six Black female sociologists highlighted in this volume are charted to ascertain the special directions of their research, which they have used as a tool for social change. In each case, an attempt is made to demonstrate their intellectual and academic evolution as they built their careers in the discipline of sociology and beyond. Further, the work attempts to enable an understanding of how their sociologies extended the very definition of the sociological enterprise by their movements between academic sociology and non-academic organizations, various social movements, and non-academic employment. The characteristics of these sociologists facilitate our understanding of how each, in her own unique way, remains true to historic politically-engaged scholarship which has been central to Black Sociology.

Appendix A

Aged Blacks: A Potpourri in the Direction of the Reduction of Inequities*

Jacquelyne J. Jackson

Among the earliest gerontological papers on black aged were probably three first appearing in *Phylon*.[1] Since then such papers have multiplied, but this proliferation has failed to produce sufficient interest in improving the objective social conditions *(e.g.,* income, housing, and transportation) of black aged, nor has it aided those experiencing involuntary relocation in the onslaught of urban renewal and highway programs. These are serious problems.

This paper focuses specifically upon (a) grandparental roles in a contemporary urban Southern setting and certain implications of those roles relative to sociocultural conditions of aged blacks; (b) the National Caucus on the Black Aged, a group recently developed to focus attention and action upon significant service, training, and research gaps relative to black aged; and (c) a specific proposal to reduce the minimum age-eligibility requirements for Old-Age, Survivors, Disability, and Health Insurance (OASDHI) for blacks, so as to reflect the racial disparities in life-expectancy rates. These three facts, interfaced in highlighting racial inequities, are set forth below.

GRANDPARENTAL ROLES AMONG SOUTHERN BLACKS

Perhaps the most impressive finding about the black grandparental roles is their striking similarity to comparable findings about non-black grandparent-grandchild patterns. If so, the emphasis often placed upon the "peculiarity" of "Black Grannies" may be unwarranted or unduly exaggerated. These findings tend to be in general agreement, *e.g.,* with those of Shanas, *et al.*[2] Shanas and Streib,[3] Townsend,[4] and Young and Wilmott[5]

53

in such areas as (1) emphasis upon the usually vivid presence of grandmothers especially in kinship networks, with an important task being involvement in grandchild rearing; (2) more involvement of grandmothers than grandfathers in activities with grandchildren; (3) closer bonds among grandmothers, daughters, and grandchildren than among grandfathers, sons, and grandchildren; and (4) the presence of extended or three-generational families within urban areas.

Frazier's classic description of "Granny: The Guardian of the Generations" depicted an energetic, courageous, and devoted "Granny" whose prestige and importance were great during and after the Civil War. "Granny" continued watching "over the destiny of the Negro families as they have moved in ever increasing numbers to the cities during the present century," wrote Frazier, with the gradual increase in patriarchal authority in family relations and in female economic subordination, decreasing "Granny's" prestige and importance. Frazier made no explicit mention of grandfathers.[6] A majority of the grandmother subjects in this study still resemble Frazier's "Granny." Grandmothers are still generally more important than grandfathers, but the importance of the latter within black urban kinship systems is increasing, necessitating a reassessment of black families and a burial of extant myths.

Kahana and Kahana[7] noted that most grandparental studies focused only upon them rather than upon both them and their grandchildren. This section is traditional in focusing upon grandparental perceptions only, but a traditional in focusing upon black grandmothers and grandfathers. Specifically, analytical data about *interactional* and *subjective* roles between (a) grandparents residing in predominantly low-income, urban renewal areas and the grandchildren they see most often, and (b) selected comparisons of the grandparental subgroupings are presented.

The subgroupings of the sampled 68 black grandparents, whose ages, marital statuses, and subgroupings are detailed in Table A.1 below, were as follows: (1) by sex, grandmothers and grandfathers; (2) by age, younger (*i.e.,* under 50 years) and older (*i.e.,* 50+ years); and (3) by household composition, grandparents living alone and grandparents not living alone. No significant age differences characterized the latter subgroup. Using t, both the grandfathers and older grandparents were significantly older than their subgroup counterparts ($p<.001$). The subjects reported approximately (a few were imprecise) 391 grandchildren, about 5.8 grandchildren per subject. Almost 12 percent had no granddaughters; almost 15 percent no grandsons. Table A.2 contains selected background information of these grandchildren.

A modified form of the Adams Kinship Schedule[8] was used to collect data in personal interview settings within the subject's homes. Following Adams (1968)[9], *interactional characteristics* referred to the "frequency of interaction and kinds of or occasions for interaction with" grandchildren, including telephone contacts and letter writing, or the non-face-to-face means of keeping in touch." His eight "contact types" (*i.e.,* home visiting, social activities, voluntary organizations, working together at the same occupation and location, rituals, communication, aid received from a specific relative, and aid given to a specific relative) were modified to seven: home visiting, social activities (including reading), church, luxury gifts, communication, aid received from grandchildren, and aid given to grandchildren. The subjective characteristics were affectional closeness, value consensus, identification, and obligation.

Determination of affectional closeness is in answer to the question: "How close would you say you feel to your . . . ?" Responses of "quite close" and "extremely close" are combined and designated as strong feelings of closeness. Value consensus is ascertained by the following question: "Do you and your. . . agree in your ideas and opinions about the things *you* consider really important in life?" Answers of "yes, completely," and "yes, to a great extent" appear to indicate substantial value consensus, as distinct from value divergence. Idealization of or identification with the relative is determined by responses to this question: "Would you like to be the kind of person your . . . is?" Close identification is

Table A.1.   Black Grandparental Subgroupings by Age and Sample Size

	Age (in years)		
SUBGROUPING	*N*	*X*	*s*
By sex:			
All grandmothers	54	59.4	13.6
Older, with spouse	6	66.7	7.5
Older, without spouse	33	66.5	7.6
Younger, with spouse	3	45.0	0.0
Younger, without spouse	12	40.0	6.7
Employed	9	49.4	12.4
Nonemployed	45	61.4	13.0
All grandfathers			
Older, with spouse	14	69.3	7.8
Older, without spouse	5	73.0	4.5
Employed	4	62.5	9.6
Nonemployed	10	72.0	4.8
By living arrangements:			
All grandparents			
Living alone	26	64.2	11.6
Not living alone	38	59.7	13.7
By age:			
Younger grandparents	15	41.0	6.4
Older grandparents	53	67.2	7.7

*No grandfathers were under 50 years of age.

Table A.2. Background Data on Grandchildren by Grandparental Subgroups

CHARACTERISTIC*	Percent Base:	GRANDPARENTAL SUBGROUPS					
		Grandmothers (N = 54)* 100.0	Grandfathers (N = 14)* 100.0	Grandparents Living		Grandparents	
				Alone Not (N = 26)* 100.0	Alone (N = 38)* 100.0	Younger 100.0	Older 100.0
		Percentage	Percentage	Percentage	Percentage	Percentage	Percentage
Number of grandsons:							
none		14.3	37.5	13	16.7	23.1	19.2
one		16.3	0.0	8.7	13.3	30.8	7.7
two		18.4	18.8	30.4	13.3	15.4	19.2
three+		51.0	43.8	47.8	56.7	30.8	53.8
Number of granddaughters:							
none		21.6	31.3	30.4	16.1	15.4	25.9
one		21.6	18.3	30.4	16.1	15.4	22.2
two		9.8	6.3	8.7	12.9	15.4	7.4
three+		47.1	43.8	30.4	54.8	53.8	44.4
Grandchildren's residence:							
in the same household as grandparent		30.4	0.0	0.0	34.5	46.2	16.7
in same city as grandparent		37.0	40.0	52.4	27.6	38.5	37.5
in northeastern states		19.6	40.0	38.1	20.7	15.4	14.6
elsewhere		13.0	20.0	9.5	17.2	0.0	31.3
Ages of grandchildren:							
under six years		25.6	14.3	14.3	29.6	58.3	13.3
6-11 years		27.9	42.9	33.3	25.9	25.0	33.3
12-17 years		20.9	28.6	19.0	29.6	8.3	26.7
18+ years		25.6	14.3	33.3	14.8	8.3	26.7
Grandchildren's marital status:							
married		41.2	33.3	62.5	22.2	0.0	44.4

Percentages were computed upon available responses, so N is sometimes less than given.

based upon the responses "yes, completely," and "in most ways." Feelings of obligation are ascertained. . . by asking . . . how important certain reasons for keeping in touch are in relation to a particular relative.[10]

FINDINGS

In general, when the data were controlled for grandparents with at least one son with offspring and at least one daughter with offspring, who either both resided elsewhere (*i.e.,* not within the same locality as the subject) or within the same location as did the subject, the grandchild seen most often was the daughter's, as opposed to the son's, child, a finding consistent with Young and Willmott's observation that grandchildren usually interact more frequently with their mother's mother than with their father's mother.[11] Rare exceptions in this sample were among subjects whose son's offspring resided with them.

Interactional characteristics. Possible responses for frequency of interaction between a grandparent and grandchild ranged from daily through "never during the past year." Percentage data in Table A.3 depict frequency of interaction in five "contact types" for subjects interacting at least "once during the year" with the grandchild.

Grandparental subgroupings emerged. Younger grandparents, grandparents living alone, and grandmothers were more likely to report home visiting than were their respective counterparts, true even when the data were controlled to exclude grandparents and grandchildren in the same household. Those living alone and those not living alone differed since the latter reported greater frequency of contact ($p < .05$).

The modal form of interaction in social activities was "shopping, exclusive of grocery shopping," with joint movie attendance especially rare. Reading was largely restricted to interaction with preschool grandchildren. Table A.4 contains a rank ordering, in decreasing frequency, of these activities.

The data on church revealed that older grandparents, grandparents living alone, and grandfathers reported less frequent church activities (most often joint attendance at regular Sunday morning worship services) with grandchildren than their counterparts. Younger grandparents were far more likely to be accompanied by or to accompany a grandchild to church than were older grandparents ($p < .05$), attributable partially to greater shared residence among the former. Joint church activity decreased as the ages of the grandparents and grandchildren increased.

Excepting younger grandparents, subjects reported infrequent or no luxury gift-giving to their grandchildren, a finding explicable perhaps by such vari-

Table A.3. Responses to Interactional Items by Grandparental Subgroups

| | | | | GRANDPARENTAL SUBGROUPS | | | |
| | | | | Grandparents Living | | Grandparents | |
CHARACTERISTIC*	Percent Base:	Grandmothers 100.0	Grandfathers 100.0	Alone 100.0	Not Alone 100.0	Younger 100.0	Older 100.0
		Percentage	Percentage	Percentage	Percentage	Percentage	Percentage
Frequency of contact with grandchild:							
daily, same household		29.3	0.0	0.0	32.0	50.0	15.9
monthly, or more often		43.9	53.8	60.0	36.0	40.0	47.7
at least once during past year		24.4	30.8	35.0	24.0	10.0	29.5
not at all during past year		2.4	15.4	5.0	8.0	0.0	6.8
Home visiting:							
yes		31.3	27.3	42.1	11.8	60.0	26.3
no		68.8	72.7	57.9	88.2	40.0	73.7
Social activities:							
going to the park		22.0	15.4	10.0	20.0	36.4	16.3
attending the movies		4.8	0.0	0.0	3.8	0.0	4.5

grocery shopping	35.7	15.0	42.3	54.5	25.0
shopping, other than grocery	45.2	30.0	46.2	63.6	31.8
local or other trips/vacation	28.6	15.0	26.9	27.3	22.7
reading	14.3	5.0	11.5	18.2	11.4
church	45.2	35.0	42.3	72.7	31.8
Luxury gifts:					
yes	32.4	15.8	47.4	75.0	23.7
no	67.6	84.2	52.6	25.0	76.3
Communication:					
S writes out of town grandchild	28.6	27.3	33.3	0.0	28.6
S written by out of town grandchild	53.3	58.3	30.0	0.0	47.8
no telephone communication on					
special occasions or emergencies	42.3	31.3	38.9	0.0	42.4
telephone communications monthly					
or more frequently	15.4	25.0	16.7	14.3	21.2

*All percentage based upon interaction having occurred at least once during the past year.

Table A.4. Rank Order of the Frequency of Social Activities between Grandparents-Grandchildren

| | | | RANK ORDER* | | | |
| | | | Grandparents Living | | Grandparents | |
Social Activity	Grandmothers	Grandfathers	Alone	Not Alone	Younger	Older
Shopping other than grocery shopping	1	2	1	1	1	1
Grocery shopping	2	2	2.5	2	2	2
Going to the park and/or walking	4	2	4	4	3	4
Movies	6	6	6	6	6	6
Trips/vacations	3	4.5	2.5	3	4	3
Reading	5	4.5	5	5	5	5

*1 = greatest frequency of occurrence; 6 = least occurring activity.

ables as (a) a greater likelihood of younger grandparents being employed; and (b) greater likelihood of grandparents providing younger grandchildren with luxury gifts and older ones with practical gifts.

Non-face-to-face communication patterns investigated were (a) telephoning grandparent-grandchild contacts; and (b) written communication among grandparent-grandchild pairs not residing within the same city. No more than one third of any grandparent subgroup reported writing to a grandchild within the preceding year. More had received correspondence from their grandchildren. Grandfathers, as well as grandparents living with others, were less likely to have had telephonic communication with grandchildren than grandmothers and grandparents living alone, but the differences were insignificant. Older grandparents were significantly more likely than younger grandparents to have such interaction ($p<.05$), an artifact, perhaps of more grandchildren living with younger grandparents. While few subjects reported relatively frequent (i.e., monthly or more often) telephone contact, most reported at least one call (usually an emergency or a "special occasion" day) during the preceding year.

Table A.5 contains responses concerning grandparent-grandchild aid patterns. A minority perceived their grandchildren as "not much help at all," a statement verbalized most often by grandfathers (50 percent), and less often by those who were living alone (37 percent), older (33 percent), living alone (28 percent), grandmothers (25 percent), and younger (20 percent). But inquiry about specific aid revealed that a majority had received assistance from grandchildren during the preceding year. Their modal responses were not instrumentally, but affectively, oriented: disregarding the "not much help at all response," the modal response for younger grandparents and grandparents living alone was "visits"; for the remaining subgroups, "A feeling of usefulness." Those living alone received more visits from grandchildren than those not living alone ($p<.05$), while the latter received greater assistance with household and/or yard chores ($p<.05$) than the former. Younger grandparents also received more chore assistance than older grandparents ($p<.05$), and more advice from grandchildren as well ($p<.05$).

The modal form of grandparent-grandchild assistance was childcare; almost 44 percent of the grandmothers, 56 percent of grandparents living with others, and 82 percent of the younger grandmothers, had grandchildren residing with them. A smaller proportion of the subjects "babysat" with school-age children awaiting parental arrival at residences other than those of the grandparents. Younger, as contrasted with older, grandparents provided more direct financial assistance to a grandchild and/or his parents ($p<.01$); they were also more involved in patterns of luxury and practical gift-giving to grandchildren

Table A.5. Mutual Aid Patterns between Grandchildren and Grandparents

| | | | GRANDPARENTAL SUBGROUPS | | | |
| | | | Grandparents Living | | Grandparents | |
CHARACTERISTIC*	Grandmothers	Grandfathers	Alone	Not Alone	Younger	Older
	Percentage	Percentage	Percentage	Percentage	Percentage	Percentage
Aid received from grandchild:						
daily, same household	29.3	0.0	0.0	32.0	50.0	15.9
financial assistance	12.5	0.0	10.5	11.8	20.7	7.9
feeling of usefulness	35.3	36.4	26.3	42.1	57.1	31.6
house or yard chores	27.8	18.2	5.3	35.0	55.6	18.6
visiting	31.3	27.3	42.1	11.8	60.0	26.3
transportation	6.5	0.0	5.3	6.3	0.0	5.3
gifts	18.8	9.1	15.8	23.5	20.0	15.8
advice	12.5	9.1	10.5	11.8	40.0	7.9
writing letters, reading, etc.	3.1	0.0	0.0	5.9	0.0	2.6
"not much help at all"	25.0	50.0	27.8	36.8	20.0	33.3
Aid given to grandchildren:						
indirect financial assistance	15.2	0.0	0.0	17.6	50.0	5.3
direct financial assistance	30.6	18.2	15.8	40.0	75.0	17.9
necessary gifts	33.3	9.1	10.5	89.5	66.7	18.4
housing	36.8	27.3	15.0	42.9	66.7	27.5
assistance with illness	11.8	9.1	0.0	16.7	16.7	10.3
child care	43.6	9.1	5.3	56.5	81.8	23.1
took grandchild on a special trip	6.3	10.0	0.0	5.9	20.0	5.4
advice	52.8	33.3	42.1	42.9	75.0	42.5
keeping after school until parent arrives	8.8	9.1	0.0	15.8	16.7	7.7
other	14.3	0.0	16.7	10.5	0.0	14.8

*All percentages based upon interaction having occurred at least once during the past year.

(p<.01), childcare (p<.001), and housing (p<.05). Grandmothers were more involved as childcare agents than grandfathers (p<.05), as were grandparents not living alone compared with those living alone (p<.001). Among the latter sub grouping, those not living alone tended to engage in greater luxury and necessary gift-giving as well (p<.05).

While impressionistic judgments suggested that the older grandparents had been far more active in grandchild rearing earlier, it was quite clear that grandparental involvement in childrearing is directly related to the grandchild's familial structure: grandparental involvement, as Frazier[12] indicated, increased with the absence of the grandchild's parent.

Subjective characteristics. Qualitative data on affectional closeness, value consensus, identification with grandchild, satisfaction of present contact with grandchild, and the primary initiant of grandparent-grandchild contacts were available for analysis. A majority of the subjects verbalized strong affectional closeness between themselves and their grandchildren. Only grandmothers considered themselves significantly closer to grandchildren than did grandfathers (p<.05), but grandparents living with others and younger grandparents tended to report greater closeness than their counterparts, suggesting probably the importance of considering more closely sex, age, and residential proximity in future grandparent-grandchild studies.

Value divergence was more typical than substantial value consensus, but the greatest congruence of value consensus between grandparents and grandchildren was found among grandfathers, which warrants an investigation of black generational transmission of political socialization and advocates for the aged. Older grandmothers displayed the most distance in grandchild-grandparent value consensus. In addition, less than five percent of the subjects closely identified with grandchildren. Almost 20 percent rejected any close identification (*i.e.,* they would not like to resemble the grandchild in any way).

Obligatory kinship ties were apparent. Most subjects, and particularly younger grandparents and grandparents living with others, felt that the obligation of "keeping in touch" was very important. Excepting younger grandparents, all of the subjects placed greater emphasis upon the obligatory than upon the enjoyable aspect of "keeping in touch." Older grandparents and those living alone desired greater grandchild contact. Compared with their respective counterparts, they were significantly less likely to be satisfied with the present contact levels (p<.05). A very small percentage of older grandparents (2 percent) and grandparents not living alone (4 percent), however, felt that less frequent grandchild contact would be desirable.

Most subjects felt that grandchildren should live near (but not necessarily with) their grandparents, and provided rationalizations categorized as unilateral and bilateral need-fits (*e.g.,* "Grandchildren can be a lot of help to their grandparents," "Grandparents can help parents with children," and "Because we need each other") and kinship obligations (*e.g.,* "Everyone should be close around their family"). Equally important, almost 15 percent of the subjects feeling that grandchildren should not live near grandparents cited the necessity for physical generational separation so as to reduce problems for the grandparent (e.g., "Do not want to be worried with them") and/or the grandchild (*e.g.,* "It tends to spoil the child") and emphasized parental responsibility. Almost 25 percent of the subjects stressed the primary responsibility of parents for rearing their own children in neolocal residences. Most were specifically concerned about possible detrimental effects of extremely close grandparent-grandchild residential proximity upon development of independence in a maturing grandchild; and, to a less extent, childrearing roles constraining grandparents with "other fish to fry," as they develop or maintain new roles as they aged.

In general, grandchildren were not considered the initiants of the grandparent-grandchild contacts. Grandfathers also did not perceive themselves in this role, but considered a parent of the grandchild as the primary contact agent for them. Younger grandparents and grandparents living alone rarely regarded themselves as prime contact agents either, inasmuch as those younger grandparents with spouses felt that the spouses actually initiated the contact most often, and both groups felt that their own children also served as links between themselves and grandchildren. Younger grandparents and grandfathers, however, were more likely to telephone a grandchild than the reverse, whereas grandchildren were more likely to contact grandmothers, older grandparents, and grandparents not living alone. The only significant subgroup distinction occurred in that grandfathers were more frequent initiators of telephone calls with grandchildren than were grandmothers ($p < .05$).

DISCUSSION

Apparently these grandparents prefer children's children to live near, but not with, them, and younger to older grandchildren.[13] Very old grandparents appeared more concerned about proximity in the event grandchildren were needed for instrumental and affective support. Relationships among affectional closeness, value consensus, and identification were unclear, but they are probably related to such preferences as those mentioned above. Any postulation of a "generation gap" per se between black grandparents and their grandchildren is too vague. That is, far greater specificity and empirical data about those gaps which may exist are needed, with particular emphasis upon separation of spurious or superficial gaps (*e.g.,* clothing or hairstyles) and substantial ones (*e.g.,* divergence upon dominant values). Age is not a sufficient explication of generation gaps in dominant values.

The specific contact types investigated suggested relatively infrequent grandchild-grandparent interaction, due perhaps to an artifact of the study in focusing directly upon those rather than upon other contact types, and/or to such variables as inadequate income, transportation, and awareness of or free and friendly access to available resources. The general findings clearly point up some problem areas, a specific one being public housing.

In this connection, empirical data on relationships between housing and kinship patterns among blacks are clearly warranted. For example, grandparent-grandchild patterns may be affected positively and negatively by public housing policies for the aged. For blacks at least, alternative forms of housing (e.g., age-segregated and age-integrated) within the same locale are desirable. Telephone service should be available. Single blacks dependent upon public housing (and especially when such dependence is fostered through their involuntary relocation as a result of urban renewal and highway express programs) should not be forced (as is true in some localities) to accept one-room or efficiency apartments, but should be permitted to occupy at least one-bedroom apartments, if they prefer such an arrangement. Physical space permitting brief or extended visits from relatives should be available.

These findings about black grandparents and their grandchildren help to debunk myths of the deaths of the "Black Grannies"; the "powerful matriarchies" ruled by "Black Grannies"; and the disintegrating or ephemeral kinship ties between aged and aging blacks. They indicate that many black grandparents serve as a point of anchorage for grandchildren and provide kinds of supports for them unavailable from their own parents. In that sense, the grandparents take on the responsibilities of and function as individual departments of welfare. Many black families, in all probability, adhere to familial norms characteristic of the larger culture. Finally, these data are most significant in helping to delineate the tremendous need for such an organization as that of the National Caucus On the Black Aged, to which I now turn.

THE NATIONAL CAUCUS ON THE BLACK AGED

As already indicated, the National Caucus on the Black Aged (hereafter, NCBA) is particularly concerned about dramatizing and reducing those significant gaps characteristic of services to, training for, and research about black aged (including, of course, the very significant gaps occurring in housing, inasmuch as the vast majority of aged blacks are residing within substandard housing). NCBA was organized in November, 1970, largely through the efforts of Hobart C. Jackson, Chief Administrator, Stephen Smith Geriatric Center (4400 West Griard Street, Philadelphia, Pennsylvania) and Robert A. Kastenbaum, Director, Center of Psychological Studies of Dying, Death, and Lethal Behaviors, Wayne State University (Detroit, Michigan). Its most immediate missions are (a) dramatizing the plight of aged blacks; and (b) having a significant impact upon and input into the forthcoming 1971 White House Conference on Aging. This Conference has been charged with the major responsibilities of drafting a national policy for the aged in the decade ahead.

In November, 1970, NCBA concluded its organizational meeting by forwarding a telegram to President Richard M. Nixon. That communication:

(1) Calls upon President Nixon and Secretary Romney (HUD) "to develop plans by November, 1971 for correcting and replacing the deteriorated housing in which 75 percent of aged Blacks live": and for maintaining home ownership among the Black Aged. (2) Calls upon President Nixon and Secretary Richardson (HEW) to develop by November, 1971 plans for moderate, liveable income for the .aged-an income meeting Bureau of Labor Statistics standards. (3) Calls upon President Nixon and the administration's Special Assistant on Aging to develop proposals by November, 1971 for nondiscriminating programs and services including adequate transportation and police protection for aged blacks. (4) Calls upon the President to direct all states of the union to go directly to the Black Aged for their ideas, recommendations, and preferences as a preparation for the White House Conference on Aging that has been projected for late 1971. (5) Calls upon the President to see that the Black Aged are adequately represented at the White House Conference by requiring each state to select at least 30 percent of their delegations from among blacks. (6) Calls upon the Predient and Secretary Richardson to increase substantially the numbers of black trained professionals and paraprofessionals in the fields of geriatrics and gerontology.[14]

Dramatization of the plight of the black aged may proceed in a number of directions. Suggestions include much individual and group support of the above objectives. Programs may be developed within academic institutions, local communities, professional and other organizations, and at whatever levels feasible in garnering support. Perhaps special emphasis might be placed upon income, health, housing, and transportation inasmuch as these usually rank high among problem areas specified by blacks themselves.

Those planning the 1971 White House Conference on Aging have designated nine "need areas" for concentration for policy recommendations in developing a national policy for the aged: (1) income; (2) housing; (3) health; (4) nutrition; (5) education; (6) transportation; (7) retirement roles and activities; (8) spiritual well-being; and (9) employment and retirement. Specialists on aging were involved in the preparation of background or position papers focusing upon the current statuses of these need areas as they related to (a) services, facilities, and programs; (b) planning and evaluation; (c) training; (d) research and demonstration; and (e) government and nongovernment organizations.

Technical committees were appointed to examine and act upon these position papers and were mandated to isolate the major issues for discussion by delegates to the Community, State and National Conferences on Aging. In addition, national organizations throughout the United States were asked to send representatives to the National Organizations' Task Forces to assist in making policy recommendations on these need areas, and during the spring of 1971, a number of local conferences and regional hearings on aging occurred. In most states, the month of May was set aside for the State House Conference on Aging, from which policy recommendations would also be channeled to the National Conference.[15]

For the most part, black representation on these various levels, including those requested to prepare position papers, those invited to participate actively in organizing and planning the various conferences, *und so weiter*, has been small. One of the ways in which NCBA envisioned itself as having an impact upon the White House Conference on Aging was through significant representation of blacks on the various levels leading up to and through the National Conference. Thus, as noted in the telegram content referred to earlier, NCBA was very much concerned about each governor in each state including at least 30 percent black representation among the State Delegates to the National Conference. Some governors explicitly received specific requests to this effect. Greater assistance in insuring the implementation of this goal was needed in every state. Assistance is yet invaluable in helping to provide realistic policy recommendations to reduce racial inequities confronting black aged in particular und the aged in general.

NCBA certainly recognizes the need for increased development of black aging specialists and is very much concerned about further utilization and expansion of opportunities leading to such specialization. It may also be significant that the federal funding programs underwriting gerontological centers and/or special programs over the past decade have effectively excluded, for whatever reasons, black colleges and universities. Until 1971, no black institution of higher learning provided any training program in aging.[16] It is also important that increasing numbers of black students, whether students at predominantly white or predominantly black institutions, become aware of the critical needs for personnel in geriatrics and gerontology, fields which can be entered from various disciplines (*e.g.,* sociology, psychology, social work, medicine, nursing, dentistry, public administration, demography, nutrition, biology, architecture, urban planning, recreation, economics, and the ministry).

This writer, at least, is seriously concerned about "who plans the planners." Relatively few blacks occupy key positions within federal agencies underwriting the bulk of the major research, training, and service programs for the aging, including those which, on occasion, underwrite such projects involving black subjects. There is a significant need for an enlargement of the pool of black policymakers within the three major branches of the federal government, as well as of policymakers, irrespective of race, who are concerned about the reduction of inequities confronting black and other aged minorities (e.g., American Indians, Mexican-Americans). The greater presence of such policymakers may be of significant value in gaining enactment of my proposal to reduce minimum age-eligibility for OASDHI so as to reflect the disproportionate racial life expectancies.

REDUCTION OF MINIMUM AGE-ELIGIBILITY REQUIREMENTS, OASDID

It has elsewhere been noted that inasmuch as blacks tend to die earlier and to perceive of themselves as being old earlier chronologically than do whites, some structural modification in the current system of determining minimum age-eligibility requirements for Old-Age Survivors, Disability, and Health Insurance (OASDHI) may be useful in reducing certain specific racial disparities."[17] In 1968, it was specifically proposed that:

> The minimum age-eligibility for retirement benefits should be racially differentiated to reflect present racial differences in life expectancies. Remaining life expectancies at age 45 may be an appropriate base for computing such differentials.[18]

In December, 1970, the following resolution was submitted to President Richard M. Nixon for consideration:

> WHEREAS available data (Herman B. Brotman: Useful Facts #19, Life Expectancy, National and by State, 1959–1961, Administration on Aging Memorandum, HEW, Washington, D.C., April 1967) indicate that nonwhites, on the average, can expect to live fewer years than is true of whites (e.g., for those born in 1900–1902, at birth, nonwhite males could expect to live 15.7 years fewer than could white males, and nonwhite females could expect to die 16.0 years earlier than could white females; and, for those born in 1959–1961, nonwhite males, on the average, could expect to die 6.1 years earlier than white males, and

nonwhite females could expect to die 7.7 years earlier than while females); AND WHEREAS the present Social Security legislation fails to consider this racial differential in life expectancy in determining the minimum age eligibility required for qualification for Social Security benefits earned by workers; AND WHEREAS nonwhites are therefore discriminated against in being denied a proportionate number of years to receive such benefits as are eligible whites; BE IT THEREFORE RESOLVED THAT the minimum age-eligibility for such retirement benefits should be racially differentiated to reflect present racial differences in life expectancies so as to reduce the discriminatory gaps in earned benefits which now occur; AND BE IT THEREFORE RESOLVED THAT the 1971 While House Conference on Aging will include this recommendation as one of its recommendations forwarded to the Congress of the United States and to appropriate federal agencies for action thereupon to institute legislatively minimum age-requirements reflecting such differences in life expectancy by race.[19]

Such a proposal has generated some interest; it has also raised some issues. In general, the issues raised have focused upon (a) the historical coverage of black workers under social insurance and demographic factors related to black aged; (b) the ethnicity and/or feasibility of excluding other significant minority groups from the initial proposal; (c) the specific fact that black beneficiaries may tend to receive proportionately more benefits, as compared with payments, than do white beneficiaries; .and (d) refinement of the specific proposal, including a more precise specification of the methodology to be employed in determining racially differentiated, minimum age-eligibility requirements.

Historical background of coverage of black workers under Social Security. As Schiltz has explained quite cogently, old-age insurance is based "at least loosely on the insurance principle, while old-age assistance is usually perceived as a public assistance program." The critical difference between the two programs is located "either in the criteria for determining the benefit amount or in the method of financing." Old-age insurance is social insurance "because the benefit level is related to previous wage history, and all participants are entitled to benefits, whether or not they are in need," and "because the costs of the program are borne by employer-employee contributions." Old-age assistance, on the other hand, is public assistance in that "the benefit level must be established by the needs of the individual (a 'means test') and only those persons in need are eligible for benefits," and because it is "financed out of the general revenues of the State and Federal governments."[20] The proposal to reduce racial inequities currently encouched within existing OASDHI legislation focuses largely upon social insurance, upon that program to which blacks have contributed their own earned monies, and in which they, themselves, have earned the right to maximum beneficiary participation.

In addition, the fact that many black recipients of old-age assistance were denied participation in old-age insurance and are therefore entitled through their earned rights as well to the monies they receive should never be overlooked.

As is well known, the Social Security Act of 1935 effectively excluded a significant proportion of black workers from coverage by excluding especially agricultural and casual laborers and private household domestics. The enactment of the Federal OASI Program (effective 1 January 1940) extended such exclusion by adding to the above categories domestics employed in club, fraternity, and sorority houses on college campuses. Thus, the vast majority of employed blacks were not covered under social insurance, an obvious and highly deliberate form of employment discrimination.

The 1939 Act continued to contribute heavily towards the necessity for a number of aged blacks to rely upon old-age assistance and, thereby, to be victims of the derogatory label of "people on welfare." More significantly, such a procedure helped undoubtedly to contribute towards the disproportionate accumulation of black people on welfare, a fact often forgotten when racial comparisons of old-age assistance recipients are made.

The Social Security Act Amendments of 1946 continued racial segregation by still excluding agricultural laborers, casual laborers, and domestic servants and by maintaining age 65 as retirement age, an age at which most blacks who had even contributed to the old-age insurance coffers were themselves dead. It was not until the Acts of 1950 and 1954 that coverage was finally extended to most agricultural laborers and domestic workers (with the 1954 qualifiers including earning a minimum of $50 within a given quarter from a single domestic employer and $100 annually from an employer of agricultural laborers).

Subsequent amendments to the Social Security Act of 1935 have resulted in extended coverage to the vast majority of blacks today, and selected provisions of the coverage to which they are entitled under the Social Security Act and Act Amendments, as of 1969, are available elsewhere.[21]

DEMOGRAPHIC FACTORS

Unfortunately, detailed data in developing a national profile of black aged in 1970 are not yet available from the U.S. Bureau of the Census. However, preliminary data indicated that an increasing proportion of black aged were metropolitan dwellers and that one out of every two black aged had annual incomes at or below the poverty level. The median 1969 income for aged black males was $1,491; for females, $1,050. Approximately six percent considered themselves as unemployed members of the labor forces.[22]

In 1960, nonwhite aged constituted a proportionately larger unit of the nonwhite rural nonfarm (7.4 percent) and rural farm (6.2 percent) population than was true of the urban population of nonwhites (5.7 percent). The median age for those at least 65 years of age was about 71 years. Almost all had received less than an elementary education. Most of the males were married, living with spouse, whereas the majority of females were widowed. A larger proportion were active within the labor force in 1960 than was apparently the case in 1970. If that trend of declining participation within the labor force is valid, then it certainly provides additional rationale for the proposal at hand. There also appeared to be no significant decline in poverty among black aged during the decade.

The Ethicity and/or Feasibility of Excluding Other Significant Minority Groups

The overriding emphasis in this article upon black aged is readily explicable by two dominant factors: (a) the writer is black; and (b) her gerontological concerns have focused sharply and almost solely upon black aged. Black aged also constitute well over 90 percent of all nonwhite aged. Moreover, many gains labored for by blacks accrue to other minority groups as well. However, in terms of political and other strategy, it may be useful to extend such a proposal to incorporate other groups. Certainly American Indians and Mexican-Americans, who have even lower educational levels and life-expectancy rates than do blacks, ought to be included, and there is no objection to that (as well as the inclusion of similar groups). The issue of including women as a categorical grouping, inasmuch as women generally outlive men, may often be used merely as a "red herring," and such an inclusion is rejected. This proposal is geared only towards the reduction of racial inequities, wherein the standard for computing new minimum age-eligibility requirements would be based upon racial differences between black and white males and black and white females.

Too often in recent months especially, black caucuses involved in the very difficult tasks of improving significantly the opportunities and utilization of those opportunities for blacks have been confronted with "But what about the women?" The concern has not been with black women (a concern, incidentally, which too few black male industrial and educational recruitment agents seem to remember), but with women in general (or at least those involved in women's liberation movements). It is, in a very real sense, perhaps unfair to place the burden of liberation for all minority groups, including the aged, upon blacks, who have limited resources available and limited access to the power system. Therefore, black demands for black aged should be regarded as legitimate demands in their own right.

Racial Comparisons of Proportionate Receipt of Benefits

Much has been made of the fact that black OASDHI beneficiaries may tend to receive proportionately more benefits (as compared with actual contributions to the insurance system) than do whites. Orshansky has written that:

> Public programs are administered without respect to race and, though limited in what they pay, are relatively more generous to the aged whose previous earnings were lowest or whose current need is greatest . . . By and large, racial differences in income are less among aged persons drawing old-age, survivors, and disability insurance benefits than among those not benefitting from this income-support program.[23]

It is, of course, true that those with proportionately lower actual contributions to OASDHI do tend to receive proportionately higher benefits from OASDHI. But it is also true that a significantly larger proportion of blacks entitled to such benefits do not, as already noted, live as long as whites on the average and, therefore, they are denied the equivalent possibility of receiving benefits for a proportionately equal amount of time. A substantial number of low-income whites (who far exceed the number of low-income blacks) also receive proportionately more from OASDHI than do whites with higher lifetime earnings. What is of most importance, however, is the fact that blacks pay proportionately more into OASDHI than do whites. As an illustration, compare Worker Black A and Worker White B, with annual 1970 incomes of $7,800 and $12,000 respectively (A = .65B). Both A and B invest $390 (5 percent) of their incomes in OASDHI. That OASDHI investment of $390 = .05 of A's income and .0325 of B's income. Thus, the black worker would have invested 1.75 percent more of his income into the system than did the white worker. Thus, this proposal can be supported on the basis of greater proportionate contributions among blacks and disproportionate receipt of benefits by blacks (with the latter occurring primarily because of their earlier deaths).

Refinement of the Specific Proposal

A number of persons have suggested that the precise method of determining racially equitable benefits should be developed prior to a public presentation of the proposal. As sound as that suggestion may be, federal agencies employ a sufficient number of technicians capable of working out the details of such a proposal and implementing it, should the basic principle be accepted. The base for determining racial differences should be established at birth, inasmuch as racial differences in life expectancies, attributable to many racial differences within the socio-cultural environment, begin at or before birth (e.g., prenatal nutritional factors); and modifications might be undertaken decennially. Thus, 1910 racial life expectancy data at birth could be employed as the baseline standard for determining minimum age-eligibility requirements for OASDHI recipients, beginning 1972; 1920 data could be utilized for 1982, and so on. The chief point is that the minimum age-eligibility requirements should be lower for blacks than for whites until such time as there is no longer any difference in their life expectancies at birth; or to put it another way, where racial differences adversely affect blacks, public programs should not operate "colorblind."

SUMMARY

The triple focus of this paper was upon (a) a description and analysis of Southern urban black grandparental roles, emphasizing certain implications for current policies surrounding black aged; (b) the National Caucus on the Black Aged, stressing its urgent missions of dramatizing the plight of the black aged and having a significant impact upon the forthcoming 1971 White House Conference on Aging, where policy recommendations for the aged in the decade ahead will be formulated, as well as its general concern for increasing substantially services to, training for, and research about black aged; and (c) a specific proposal to reduce the minimum age-eligibility requirements for recipients of Old-Age, Survivors, Disability and Health Insurance (OASDHI, a form of Social Security) so as to reduce the racial inequities now extant, wherein blacks are far less likely to receive proportionate benefits as whites, even though they may be very likely to have invested proportionately more of their life-time earnings into Social Security, inasmuch as they tend to die earlier than do whites. The interfacing of these foci occurred largely in that the grandparental data point toward the need for improved economic and housing conditions for grandparents, for their children, and for their children's children. The National Caucus on the Black Aged is significantly concerned about improving these adverse conditions and, in this connection, seeks assistance from all relevant resources (including those blacks who are not yet aged). The specific proposal to realize greater racial equity between aged whites and blacks is one response to the need to improve the deplorable income plight of many black aged: in this case, a specific improvement in obtaining benefits which black aged themselves have earned. There is need for greater attention upon black aged at the three basic levels of research, training and services,[24] and it is hoped that this paper may play a small part in contributing towards the gradual increase in effective research, adequate training producing increased personnel, and, above all, meaningful services available to aging and aged blacks.

NOTES

From *Aging Black Women: Selected Readings for NCBA*. Jacquelyne J. Jackson (ed.). The National Caucus on the Black Aged: Washington, D.C., 1975, pp. 365–385. Reprinted by Permission.

* This paper was partially supported by the Center for the Study of Aging and Human Development, Duke University Medical Center, Durham, North Carolina, Grant 5 T01 HD00l64 of the National Institute of Child Health and Human Development, and by the U.S. Public Health Service Grant # MH 1655402.

1. T. Lynn Smith, "The Changing Number and Distribution of the Aged Negro Population of the United States," *Phylon*, XXVIII (Winter, 1957), 339–54; W. M. Beattie, Jr., "The Aging Negro: Some Implications for Social Welfare Services," *Phylon*, XXI (Winter, 1960), 131–35; J. Himes and M. Hamlett, "The Assessment of Adjustment of Aged Negro Women in a Southern city," *Phylon*, XXIII (Summer, 1969), 139–47.

2. Ethel Shanas, *et al.*, *Old People in Three Industrial Societies* (Chicago, 1968).

3. Ethel Shanas and Gordon Streib, *Social Structure and the Family: Generational Relations* (Englewood Cliffs, 1965).

4. Peter Townsend, *The Family Life of Old People* (London, 1957).

5. Michael Young and Peter Willmott, *Family and Kinship in East London* (London, 1957).

6. E. Franklin Frazier, *The Negro Family in the United States* (Chicago, 1939), pp. 114–24.

7. Boas Kahana and Eva Kahana, "Grandparenthood from the Perspective of the Developing Grandchild" (Mimeographed, Washington University, St. Louis, Missouri, 1969).

8. Bert N. Adams, *Kinship in an Urban Setting* (Chicago, 1958). pp. 10–14.

9. *Ibid*, pp. 13–15.

10. *Ibid,* pp. 14–15.

11. Young and Willmott. *op. cit.*

12. Frazier, *op. cit*

13. Cf., Kahana and Kahana, *op. cit.*, and also Jacquelyne J. Jackson, "Kinship Relations Among Older Negro Americans" (Paper read at the Eighth International Congress of Gerontology, Washington, D.C., August 1969); Jacquelyne J. Jackson, "Urban Negro Kinship Relations" (Paper read at the annual meeting, American Sociological Association, San Francisco, California, September, 1969); Jacquelyne J. Jackson. "Changing Kinship Roles and Patterns Among Older Persons in a Black Community" (Paper read at the annual meeting, American Psychological Association, Washington, D.C., September, 1959); Jacquelyne J. Jackson, "Kinship Relations Among Urban Blacks," *Journal of Social and Behavioral Sciences*, XVI (Winter, 1970), 1–13.

14. *The Philadelphia Tribune*, November 14, 1970, p. 21.

15. "The Year of the White House Conference on Aging," Aging, No. 195 (January, 1971).

16. In July 1971, largely through the efforts of NCBA, Fisk University was awarded a grant of about $92,000 by the Administration on Aging for such a program, leading to a master's degree in sociology.

17. Jacquelyne J. Jackson, "Aged Negroes: Their Cultural Departures from Statistical Stereotypes and Rural-Urban Differences," *The Gerontologist*, X (Summer, 1970). 140–45; and *"Letter: in Economics of Aging: Toward a Full Share in Abundance Hearing Before the Special Committee on Aging, United States Senate, Part 1-Survey Hearing, April 29–30. 1969, Washington, D.C. (U.S. Government Printing Office*, Washington, D.C. 1969), pp.313–15.

18. Jackson, "Aged Negroes," *op. cit.* p.141

19. Jacquelyne J. Jackson to President Richard M. Nixon, December, 1970.

20. Michael E. Schiltz, *Public Attitudes towards Social Security. 1935–1965*. Research Report No. 33. U.S. Social Security Administration (U.S. Government Printing Office, Washington. D.C., 1970) p.12.

21. Annual Statistical Supplement, 1968, Social Security Bulletin (U.S. Government Printing Office, Washington, D.C., 1969), pp. 10–19.

22. Mimeographed preliminary data compiled by the National Urban League for Inabel Lindsay, 1971.

23. Mollie Orshansky, "The Aged Negro and His Income," *Social Security Bulletin*, XXVII (February, 1964), 3–13.

24. Jacquelyne J. Jackson, "Social Gerontology and The Negro: A Review," *The Gerontologist*.VII (September, 1967), 168–78, and Jacquelyne J. Jackson, "Exhibit A. Negro Aged and Social Gerontology: Current Status and Some Emerging Issues," in *Long-Range Program and Research Needs in Aging and Related Fields, Hearings Before the Special Committee on Aging, United States Senate, Part I, Survey, December 5 and 6,1967*, Washington, D.C. (U.S. Government Printing Office, Washington, D.C., 1961), pp. 338–41.

Appendix B

Dialectics of Black Male-Female Relationships

La Frances Rodgers-Rose

One of the most complex and pressing issues in the struggle for Black survival is centered in and grows out of the relationship between Black men and women. This relationship, in the final analysis, determines how they support each other as men and women and how they will raise their children.

The relationship between Black men and women does not take place in a vacuum. They act out their behavior in a society which has clearly defined role behavior. Men are supposed to be aggressive, women passive. With such a definition of role behavior, based on inequality rather than equality, the relationship between men and women cannot help but be tenuous. Moreover, any male-female relationship, there are the dialectics of creation and criticism which must take place in an environment of open discussion and sociability (Foote, 1953). This chapter will attempt to look at some of the issues that confront Black men and women as they interact in a process of criticism and creation. Specifically, I will discuss some myths about Black men and women and properties of male-female relationships.

MYTHS OF THE ROLES AND RELATIONSHIPS BETWEEN BLACK MEN AND WOMEN

If a situation is defined as real, then it is real in its consequences. W.I. Thomas

Most of what we know about Black male-female relationships is a result of the biased research conducted by white social scientists. For example, we hear that in order for Black people to succeed, Black women must stand behind Black men—Black women must step back and let the Black man lead. The assumption, based on biased work of white researchers, is that Black

77

women have led their men. But any objective look at Black history will show this has never been the case. Equality between Black men and women has been misrepresented as female dominance. What has happened is that some Black men and women have internalized the myths of white social scientists, and these definitions of situations have become real in their consequences.

Another myth that some Blacks have internalized is that the Black male is shiftless, that he does not want to work, that he would rather hang on the corner than look for a job. Objective reading of Black history shows the efforts that Black men have made to find jobs—jobs that paid very little and were demeaning in nature. Yet another myth in this country is that Black women earn more money than Black men, that Black women can get jobs when Black men cannot. U.S. Census Bureau data show that this is not true, nor has it ever been true. In fact, Black woman are the lowest paid group in the country: They make less money than white men and women and Black men (Ferris, 1971:141). Black women are, in general, the most unemployed and under-employed group. (1971:302–320) A related myth is that Black women are generally more educated than Black men, and historically this has been the case. However, today this is no longer as true (1971:23).

I am suggesting that a great deal of what is happening to Black men and women as they relate to one another is a consequence of definitions based on stereotypes of Blacks or biased research, and not from the reality systems of Black men and women. Before we can move toward defining Black male and female relationships, we must expose false definitions that grow out of thought systems which serve to divide and conquer Black people. To the extent that we are unaware of these false reality systems, we will believe them, define them as real, and, as W.I. Thomas suggested, they will become real in their consequences. For example, the Black woman is seen as having certain qualities and the Black man is seen as lacking these qualities. The Black woman is seen as needing little protecting either physically or mentally, while the Black man is seen as needing both physical and mental protection—he lacks the ability to survive in the outside world. The Black woman must protect him. Further, the Black woman is seen as a dominating matriarch: She emasculates the Black man and his character becomes "feminine" in nature. He does not know what to do unless he is told by the woman.

Growing out of this myth is the further notion that most Black households are headed by women, that the male is absent from the home, and that Black children do not have male models. The reality of the situation is that two-thirds of all Black households do have both male and female present. In some households, the male is not present to be counted by the census taker. He may be absent for strategic purposes—for example, a needy mother cannot get welfare if there is a man in the home; aid is given only to dependent children, not to struggling intact families. Moreover, white social scientists ignore the fact that Black women have boyfriends, fathers, brothers, and uncles who can and do serve as role models.

Finally, the Black man and woman are defined as being sexually aggressive. White mythology has asserted that both the Black male and female are anxious to have sexual relationships with whites. The female is defined as loose in her morals and out to sell her body to the highest bidder; she wants to establish meaningless relationships with white men at the expense of the Black man. Black men seek sexual relationships with white women. Again, when we unmask the myth, we find that less than two percent of all marriages in this country are between Black and white people. When Blacks are asked to rank the priority of things they want in this country, interracial marriage is ranked last, with economic and political equality ranked first.

As can be seen from the foregoing discussion, it is easy for Black people to internalize and use such false definitions of themselves. To the extent that an individual has internalized these definitions, his/her mode of interaction with the opposite sex will be affected. Therefore, when a relationship is not going well, the individual will resort to such negative definitions and interpretations as "Black women are too independent," "Black men are too possessive," "Black men's feelings are too easily hurt," "Black women are evil," "Black women argue too much," "Black men are weak," "Black men are castrated," and "Black women don't appreciate good treatment." Moreover, these negative definitions have already been supplied and are readily available to the actor. These ready-made definitions keep Black men and women from looking inward to what they contribute to the outcome of a particular relationship. One can easily blame the other. Such myths, then, have functioned to divide Black men and women, and they have served as rationalizations for the status quo. Myths keep the individuals focused on criticism rather than on the interplay between the critical and the creative aspects of any male-female relationship.

PROPERTIES OF DIALECTIC RELATIONSHIPS BETWEEN BLACK MEN AND WOMEN

Sociologists have in many cases failed to study the depth of interpersonal relationships between the groups of people they analyze. They have, instead, tended to study the surface areas—those aspects which can be easily defined, codified, and discussed. We know a great deal about financial and sexual aspects of marriage, but we know much less about what attracts one individual to another, what people are looking for in intimate relationships, and what qualities make for viable dialectic relationships. Likewise, we find that men and women are not socialized to look for nor can they articulate their needs in terms of qualities wanted. We are taught to pay more attention to the outward characteristics of a person: education, occupation, and income. Recently, sexual compatibility has been included in these characteristics. Thus, we find people in relationships not realizing what they want from that relationship.

QUALITIES IN MALE-FEMALE RELATIONSHIPS

This chapter is based on interviews of 49 Black women and 39 Black men. The data were collected in April and May 1975.[1] Each person was asked five questions: (1) What qualities do you want in a man/woman with whom you are having an intimate relationship? (2) What behavior/action would show the above qualities? (3) What qualities do you dislike/hate in a man/woman that would make you dissolve that relationship? (4) What behavior/action would show these negative qualities? (5) If you were dating steadily, how often would you like to see that person? The responses to each of these questions were recorded verbatim. Each response was then content analyzed. Background data on age, education, occupation, and marital status were also gathered. Table B.1 shows the distribution of males and females by age groups on

Table B.1.   Distribution of Males and Females by Age Group on Specific Status Characteristics

	Females		Males	
Characteristics	Under 30 Years (N = 24)	Over 30 Years (N = 25)	Under 30 Years (N = 22)	Over 30 Years (N = 17)
Mean Age	22.8	42	22	39
Mean Education	13.6	14.4	14.8	15.3
Dates/Week	4	2.2	3.4	3.4
Marital Status				
Single	16	1	16	5
Married	3	9	6	8
Separated	3	4	0	2
Divorced	1	7	0	2
Widowed	1	3	0	0
Occupation				
Professional	8	13	8	11
Clerical/Skilled	5	6	5	3
Unskilled	0	5	1	2
Student	7	0	5	1
Housewife	2	0	0	0

specific characteristics. As one can see from Table B.1, there is a wide range and a similar age span for males and females. The educational level is above the national norm. Most are single or separated/divorced. Only 30 percent of the sample is presently married, and the professional category is overrepresented in the sample.

The following results were indicated for males and females. In the area of positive qualities, one may note from Table B.2 that females under 30 years of age say that the qualities they most want in a man are understanding, honesty, and a person who is warm and gentle. These are the global qualities; that is, qualities showing the greatest frequencies. Only qualities mentioned by at least five persons are listed in the tables which follow; however, many other qualities were given. The aim of this study was to show those qualities that have some kind of consensus among age and sex groups. Other qualities mentioned by women under 30 years of age were intelligence, sense of humor, stability, and awareness of self. Table B.2 for women over 30 indicates that the most outstanding desirable quality was honesty. This was the only global quality listed, while from women under 30, honesty and understanding had the same frequency. There is a greater consensus among females than males on the positive qualities desired in a person with whom they are having an intimate relationship. For men under 30, the quality having the greatest frequency was independence—a characteristic which men traditionally do not like to see in women. Men over 30 show a global quality of good manners; for example, they mention "acts like a lady," "has good manner of speech," and "the way she carries herself in public." This quality, proper manners, indicates the more traditional way of viewing women. Also, in viewing Table B.3, one may note that males over 30 list "character" traits of the individual rather than the "affective" qualities of the person.

When we turn to how these positive qualities are viewed in behavior, the picture changes. Here we find that women under 30 do not ask for a behavioral quality paralleling the qualities of understanding and honesty; rather, they say the person should be respectful and well-groomed. One must raise the following question: Is there an incongruency between stating that the most desired quality is understanding and stating that, behaviorally, one wants respect and a person who is well-groomed? One refers to effect—understanding—and the other talks about character traits—respectful. In general, males and females in this sample found it difficult to give behavioral/actions indicators than general qualities. And in several cases there were people who listed general qualities as behavior/action. It would seem that this is the area in which one needs to be able to identify the action that shows love. As Foote (1953) suggested, love is known by its works. It is an activity, a process. It is one thing to articulate qualities, but an entirely different thing to know that a certain behavior/action is love.

Table B.2.   Positive Qualities Wanted in a Male by Black Females

I. Black Females Under 30 (N = 24)

A. Global Qualities
  1. Ideas
       Aware of Self (6)
       Black Identity (6)
       Independent (6)
  2. Affectivity/Character
       Understanding (14)
       Honesty (14)
       Warm/gentle (10)
  3. Character I
       Intelligent (8)
       Sense of humor (8)
       Positive self-concept (8)
       Stable (8)
  4. Character II
       Nice looking (7)
       Generous (7)

B. Behavioral Global Qualities
  1. Ideas
       Specific goals (7)

  2. Character
       Respectful (11)
       Well-groomed (11)

  3. Affective
       Good lover (7)
       Responds to my needs (7)
       Encourages me (6)

II. Black Females Over 30 (N = 25)

A. Global Qualities
  1. Affectivity
       Understanding (9)
       Aware of my needs (9)
       Affectionate (8)
       Aware of others (7)
  2. Character I
       Honesty (16)
  3. Character II
       Dependable (6)
       Down-to-earth (7)
       Handsome (5)
  4. Character III
       Intelligent (10)
       Ambitious (11)

B. Behavioral Global Qualities
  1. Affectivity
       Sharing (6)
       Kind to others (6)

  2. Affectivity
       Sexually compatible (6)
  3. Affectivity
       Open communication (15)

  4. Affectivity
       Takes me where he goes (10)
       Gives self according to my needs (11)

To summarize, for women over 30 years we find a consistency in the qualities wanted, "honesty," and the behavior indicated is "open communication." Women over 30 indicate affective behavioral qualities, while women under 30 consider character traits. For men in both age groups there is also a consistency of qualities and behavior. The males under 30 says they want a woman who is "calm"—cool in her behavior, one who is doing something to better herself, such as going to school or being employed. There are behavioral indicators of independence. Males over 30 say they want a woman who has "proper manners"; behaviorally, the global quality is "knowing when to listen," an indicator of proper manners.

In general, there seems to be a distinct difference among the four age groups on the qualities wanted in an intimate relationship. This is true particularly for the global qualities. However, in looking at the various qualities

Table B.3. Positive Qualities Wanted in a Female by Black Males

I. Black Males Under 30 (N = 22)

A. Global Qualities
  1. Affectivity
    Loving/tender (13)
    Understanding (10)
    Considerate (6)
    Faithful (6)
  2. Character I
    Independent (17)

  3. Character II
    Honest (13)
    Clean and neat (11)
    Beautiful (7)
  4. Character III
    Strong self-concept (10)
    Aware of self (8)
    Intelligent (11)
  5. Character IV
    Open-minded (9)
    Respectful of others (5)

B. Behavioral Global Qualities
  1. Affectivity
    Takes care of my needs (6)
    Sexually compatible (6)

  2. Character I
    Manners (9)
    Calm (10)
    Going to school/employed (9)
  3. Character II
    Independent action (7)

II. Black Males Over 30 (N = 17)

A. Global Qualities
  1. Affectivity/Character
    Understanding (8)
    Honest (8)
    Sensitive (7)
    Tender and kind (7)
  2. Character I
    Proper manners (17)
  3. Character II
    Clean and neat (8)
    Independent (8)
    Intelligent (5)
  4. Character III
    Loyal (7)
    Dependable (6
    Open and truthful (6)

B. Behavioral Global Qualities
  1. Affectivity
    Sexually compatible (4)
    Kissing, holding, responding to me (4)

  2. Character I
    Knowing when to listen (9)
  3. Character II
    Active in sports (4)

wanted, there is indeed overlap. But the significant point is the priority given the different qualities. It would seem that Black males and females differ among themselves and also within groups. In fact, a review of Tables B.2 and B.3 seems to suggest that females over 30 have more in common with males under 30, and that females under 30 have more in common with males over 30. A larger sample is needed before we can be sure of this possible relationship.

When we turn to the negative qualities and behaviors disliked in a man/woman, we find that women were able to list more negative qualities disliked in males than vice versa. Whereas females have at least seven negative qualities, males only have four areas of negative qualities. Females under 30 say they dislike a male who dominates or who is selfish and dependent, while females over 30 say they dislike a male who is immature and dishonest. Here again we see a consistency in females over 30 in the things they like in a male ("honesty") and the things they dislike in a male ("dishonesty"). This consistency across positive and negative qualities is only true for this age and sex group. For males under 30, the qualities disliked—again, similar to females over 30—were dishonesty and a person who is unaffectionate. Males over 30 showed less of a consensus than any other age or sex group. The highest frequency for any quality disliked was listed by only five people. Here they list disrespectfulness, rigidity, irresponsibility, and dishonesty. Although listed as global qualities, these are not global in the same sense as other tables showing global qualities. Looking at the behavioral qualities disliked, we find that males over 30 and females under 30 both mention lying as the behavior most disliked. For women over 30, physical violence is most disliked, and for males under 30 it is a person who is unclean and one who cheats (runs around with other men).

It is interesting to note that in listing the qualities liked or the qualities disliked in intimate relationships the traditional variables that sociologists use in studying marriage and the family are not shown. That is, in the global qualities shown no 0ne mentioned occupation, income, education, or sexual compatibility. But rather, qualities dealt more with the inner person—his/her character or the affective aspects of the person.

This preliminary study indicates that if we are to begin to understand the relationship between Black men and women, or for that matter women and men in general, we must move beyond the outer status of the person to the inner qualities of the person. When given an open-ended, unstructured question on the qualities liked and the qualities disliked in intimate relationships, this sample of Black men and women showed that they are concerned with qualities such as understanding, honesty, warmth, dress, respectability, open communication, sharing, independence, listening capability, dominance, selfishness, lying, unfaithfulness, immaturity, physical violence, lack of affection, and uncleanliness.

Research along this line will add to our knowledge of the relationship between Black men and women. Further, I feel that what is true for Black men and women will also be true for men and women in general. That is, people are concerned with intangible, hard-to-analyze qualities in a relationship rather than outward status variables. It remains to be seen whether Blacks and

Table B.4.   Negative Qualities Disliked in Males by Black Females

I. Black Females Under 30 (N = 24)	
A. Global Qualities	B. Behavioral Global Qualities
1. Character I	1. Affectivity
Dominant (14)	Sexually incompatible (5)
Selfish (14)	
Dependent (12)	
2. Character II	2. Character I
Unfaithful (8)	Lying (13)
Possessive (8)	
Dishonest (6)	
3. Character III	3. Character II
Ignorant (7)	Physical violence (9)
Immature (7)	Stay-at-home (8)
	Disrespectful (8)
	Never show/late (8)
	Lazy (7)
	Loudmouth (5)
	Drunken (5)
4. Character IV	
No patience (7)	
No self-respect (5)	

II. Black Females Over 30 (N = 25)	
A. Global Qualities	B. Behavioral Global Qualities
1. Character I	1. Character I
Immature (11)	Physically violent (13)
Dishonest (10)	
2. Character II	2. Character I
No self-respect (6)	Drunken (9)
Dependent (5)	
3. Character II	3. Character III
Ignorant (5)	Other women (7)
Selfish (5)	
4. Character III	4. Character IV
Intelligent (10)	Verbal abuse (5)
Ambitious (11)	Never show/late (5)
	Gossipy (5)
	Jealous (5)

Table B.5.   Negative Qualities Disliked in Females by Black Males

I. Black Males Under 30 (N = 22)	
A. Global Qualities Qualities	B. Behavioral Global
1. Affectivity/Character Unaffectionate (11) Dishonest (11)	1. Character Unclean (8) Clean (8)
2. Character Selfish (8) Irresponsible (8) Poor outlook on life (8)	2 Character II Lying (6) Disrespectful (5) Nags (5)

II. Black Males Over 30 (N = 17)	
A. Global Qualities Qualities	B. Behavioral Global
1. Character Disrespectful (5) Rigid (5) Irresponsible (5) Dishonest (5)	1. Character I Lying (9)
	2. Character II Curses (6) Drunken (5) Unclean (5)

other racial groups will show the same diversity as this sample, or whether a larger, more random sample will produce the same results between Black males and females. I am presently pursuing the latter question of a larger, more random sample of Black men and women.

I have attempted to show in this brief research study that sociologists who have studied relationships between males and females have failed to study the qualities wanted in persons with whom intimate relations are established. Instead, they have studied the outward special characteristics of income, education, occupation, and sexual compatibility.

NOTES

From *Black Male-Female Relationships: A Resource Book of Selected Materials*. Delores P. Aldridge (ed.). Kendall-Hunt Publishing Company: Dubuque, Iowa, pp. 223–235. Reprinted by Permission.

1. A search and referral method was used to obtain the sample. The research initially made contact with a small number of Black men and women. They in turn were

asked to refer the interviewer to another person. Interviews ranged from 45 minutes to two hours.

BIBLIOGRAPHY

Alexander, T. and S. Sillen (1972) Racism and Psychiatry. New York: Brunner-Mazel.

Anderson, C. S. and J. Himes (1969) "Dating values and norms on a Negro college campus." Marriage and Family Living 21:227–229.

Bambara, T. C. (1972) "How Black women educate each other." Sexual Behavior 2: 12–13.

Beal, F. (1969) "Double jeopardy: to be Black and female." New Generations 5: 23–28.

Bernard, J. (l966a) "Marital stability and patterns of status variables." Journal of Marriage and the Family 28: 421–439.

———. (1966b) Marriage and Family Among Negroes. Englewood Cliffs, NJ: Prentice-Hall.

Billingsley, A. (1966) Black Families in White America. Englewood Cliffs: NJ: Prentice-Hall.

———. (1969) "Family functioning in the low-income Black community." Social casework 50: 563–572.

Blood, R. and D. Wolfe (1960) Husbands and Wives: The Dynamics of Married Living. New York: Free Press.

Blumer, H. (1940) "The problem of the concept in social psychology." American Journal of Sociology 45: 707–719.

———. (1969) Symbolic Interactionism: Perspective and Method. Englewood Cliffs, NJ: Prentice-Hall.

Bond, J. and P. Berry (1974) "Is the Black male castrated?" in T. Cade (ed.) The Black Woman: An Anthology. New York: Signet.

Bradburn, N. (1969) "Working wives and marriage happiness." American Journal of Sociology 74: 392–407.

Burchinal, L. (1964) "The premarital dyad and love involvement," in H. T. Christensen (ed.) Handbook of Marriage and the Family. Chicago: Rand McNally.

Burgress, E. and P. Wallin (1953) Engagement and Marriage. Chicago: J. B. Lippincott.

Byrne, D. (1961) "Interpersonal attraction and attitude similarity." Journal of Abnormal and Social Psychology 62: 712–715.

Cooley, C. H. (1902) Human Nature and the Social Order. New York: Scribners.

Coser, R. L. [ed.] (1964) The Family: Its Structure and Functions. New York: St. Martin's Press.

Deutscher, 1. (1973) What We Say/What We Do: Sentiments and Acts. Glenview, IL: Scott, Foresman.

Donnelly, M. (1963) "Towards a theory of courtship." Marriage and Family Living 25: 290–293.

Drake, S. C. and H. Cayton (1945) Black Metropolis. New York: Harcourt Brace Jovanovich.

DuBois, W. E. B. (1903) The Souls of Black Folks. Chicago: A. C. McClury.

Edwards, G. (1963) "Marriage and family life among Negroes." Journal of Negro Education 32: 451–465.

Farley, R. (1971) "Family stability: a comparison of trends between Blacks and whites." American Sociological Review 36: 1–17.

Foote, N. (1953) "Love." Psychiatry 16: 245–251.

Frazier, E. (1939) "The Negro Family in the United States. Chicago: University of Chicago Press.

Ferris, A. L. (1971) Indicators of Trends in the Status of American Women. New York: Russell Sage.

Geismar, L. (1962) "Measuring family disorganization." Marriage and Family Living 24: 51–56.

Glaser, B. and A. Strauss (1967) The Discovery of Grounded Theory. Chicago: AVC.

Glick, P. and A. Norton (1971) "Frequency, duration and probability of marriage and divorce." Journal of Marriage and the Family 33.

Goode, W. (1956) After Divorce. New York: Free Press.

——. (1959) "The theoretical importance of love." American Sociological Review 24: 38–47.

Gorer, G. (1948) The American People: A Study in National Character. New York: W. W. Norton.

Gouldner, A. (1962) "Anti-minotaur: the myth of value free sociology." Social Problems 9: 199–213.

Habenstein, R. [ed.] (1970) Pathways to Data: Field Methods for Studying Ongoing Social Organizations. Chicago: AVC.

Hannerz, U. (1969) "The roots of Black manhood." Transaction: 6: 12–21.

Hare, N. (964) "The frustrated masculinity of the Negro male." Negro Digest 14: 5–9.

Harper, R. (1958) "Honesty in courtship." The Humanist 18: 103–107.

Harris, A. O. (1974) "Dilemma of growing up Black and female." Journal of Social and Behavioral Sciences 20: 28–40.

Hernton, C. (1965) Sex and Racism. New York: Grove Press.

——. (1974) Coming Together. New York: Random House.

Herr, D. (1958) "Dominance and the working wife." Social Forces 36: 341–347.

——. (1963) "The measurement and bases of family power." Marriage and Family Living 25: 133–139.

Herskovitz, M. (1941) The Myth of the Negro Past. New York: Harper & Row.

Herzog, E. (1966) "Is there a "breakdown' of the Negro family?" Social Work 11:3–10.

Hewitt, L. (1958) "Student perceptions of traits desired in themselves as dating and marriage partners." Marriage and Family Living 20; 349–360.

Hill, R. (1945) "Campus norms in mate selection." Journal of Home Economics 37: 554–558.

Hill, R (1972) The Strengths of Black Families. New York: National Urban League.

Hyman, H. and J. Reid (1969) "Black matriarch reconsidered: evidence from secondary analysis of sample survey." Public Opinion Quarterly 33: 346–354.

Jackson, J. (1971) "But where are the men?" The Black Scholar 2: 30–41.

——. (1973) "Black women created equal to Black men." Essence (November): 56–72.

——. (1974) "Ordinary Black husbands: the truly hidden men." Journal of Social and Behavioral Sciences 20: 19–27.

Johnson, C. S. (1934) Shadow of the Plantation. Chicago: University of Chicago Press.

Ladner, J. (1972) Tomorrow's Tomorrow: The Black Woman. New York: Doubleday.

Kamii, C. and N. Radin (1967) "Class differences in the socialization practices of Negro mothers," Journal of Marriage and the Family 29: 302–310.

King, C. (1954) "The sex factor in marital adjustment." Marriage and Family Living 16: 237–240.

King, K. (1967) "A comparison of the Negro and white family power structure in low-income families." Child and Family 6: 65–74.

Lerner, G. (1972) Black Women in White America. New York: Pantheon.

Lewis, H. (1955) Blackways of Kent. Chapel Hill: University of North carolina Press.

——. (1965) "Child rearing among low-income families," L. Ferman et al. (eds.) Poverty in America. Ann Arbor: University of Michigan Press.

——. (1967) "Culture, class, and family life among low-income urban Negroes," in A. Ross and H. Hill (eds.) Employment, Race and Poverty. New York: Harcourt Brace Jovanovich.

Liebow, E. (1967) Talley's Corner. Boston: Little, Brown.

Mack, D. (1971) "Where the Black matriarchy theorists went wrong." Psychology Today 4: 86–88.

Mannheim, K. (1936) Ideology and Utopia. New York: Harcourt Brace Jovanovich.

Maxwell, J. W. (1968) "Rural Negro father participation in family activities." Rural Sociology 33: 80–93.

Mead, G. H. (1934) Mind, Self and Society. Chicago: University of Chicago Press.

Miller, S. M. et al. (1965) "A critique of the non-deferred gratification pattern." in L. Ferman et al. (eds.) Poverty in America. Ann Arbor: University of Michigan Press.

Mills, C. W. (1940) "Methodological consequences of the sociology of knowledge." American Journal of Sociology 46: 316–330.

——. (1959) The Sociological Imagination. New York: Oxford University Press.

Morgan, R. [ed.] (1970) Sisterhood is Powerful. New York: Vintage Books.

Moynihan, D. (1965) The Negro Family: The Call for National Action. Washington, DC: Department of Labor.

Myers, L. (1975) "Black women: selectivity among roles and reference groups in maintenance of self-esteem." Journal of Social and Behavioral Sciences 21: 39–47.

Nye, F. I. (1957) "Child adjustment in broken and in unhappy homes." Marriage and Family Living 19: 356–361.

Prescott, D. (1952) "The role of love in human development." Journal of Home Economics 44: 73–176.

Parker, S. and R. Kleiner (1966) "Characteristics of Negro mothers in single-headed households." Journal of Marriage and the Family 31: 500–506.

———. (1969) "Social and psychological dimensions of the family role performance of the Negro male." Journal of Marriage and the Family 31: 500–506.

Prescott, D. (1952) "The role of love in human development." Journal of Rome Economics 44: 73–176.

Rainwater, L. (1966) "Crucible of identity," in T. Parsons and K. Clark (eds.) The Negro American. Boston: Beacon.

Reid, I. (1972) Together Black Women. New York: Emerson Hall.

Reiss, I. (1960) Premarital Sexual Standards in America. New York: Free Press.

Scanzoni, J. (1971) The Black Family in Modern Society. Boston: Allyn & Bacon.

Schulz, D. (1969) Coming Up Black: Patterns of Ghetto Socialization. Englewood Cliffs, NJ: Prentice-Hall.

Staples, R. (1970a) "The myth of the Black matriarchy." The Black Scholar 1: 2–9.

———. (1970b) "Educating the Black male at various class levels for marital roles." The Family Coordinator 30: 164–167.

———. (1971) The Black Family: Essays and Studies. Belmont, CA: Wadsworth.

———. (1972) "The sexuality of Black women." Sexual Behavior 2: 4–15.

———. (1973) The Black Woman in America. Chicago: Nelson-Hall.

Stokes, G. (1968) "Black woman to Black man." Liberator 8: 17–19.

Sullivan, H. S. (1953) The Interpersonal Theory of Psychiatry. New York: W. W. Norton.

Appendix C

Tomorrow's Tomorrow:
The Black Woman

Joyce A. Ladner

What problems face the sociologist who attempts to transcend the "liberal bourgeois" perspective in his analysis and substitute for it one that emerges from and is shaped by the Black experience? In this chapter, taken from the introduction to the anthology editor's work, *Tomorrow's Tomorrow: The Black Woman*, some basic assumptions regarding the necessity for reconceptualizing this topic are set forth.

It is very difficult to determine whether this work had its beginnings when I was growing up in rural Mississippi and experiencing all the tensions, conflicts, joys, sorrows, warmth, compassion and cruelty that was associated with *becoming a Black woman*; or whether it originated "With my graduate school career when I became engaged in research for a doctoral dissertation. I am sure that the twenty years I spent being socialized by my family and the broader Black community prior to entering graduate school shaped my perception of life, defined my emotive responses to the world and enhanced my ability to survive in a society that has not made survival for Blacks easy. Therefore, when I decided to engage in research on what approaching womanhood meant to poor Black girls in the city, I brought with me these attitudes, values, beliefs and in effect, a Black perspective. Because of this cultural sensitivity I had to the lifestyles of the over one hundred adolescent, preadolescent and adult females I "studied," I had to mediate tensions that existed from day to day between the reality and validity of their lives and the tendency to view it from the deviant perspective in "accordance with my academic training.

Deviance is the invention of a group that uses its own standards as the ideal by which others are to be judged. Howard Becker states that:

> Social groups create deviance by making the rules whose infraction constitutes deviance, and by applying these rules to particular people and labeling them as outsiders. From this point of view, deviance is not a quality of the act the person

commits, but rather a consequence of the application by others of rules and sanc-
tions to an "offender." The deviant is one to whom that label has successfully
been applied; deviant behavior is behavior that people so label.[1]

Other students of social problems have adhered to the same position.[2] Placing Black people in the context of the deviant perspective has been possible
because Blacks have not had the necessary power to resist the labels. This
power could have come only from the ability to provide the definitions of
one's past, present and future. Since Blacks have always, until recently, been
defined by the majority group, that group's characterization was the one that
was predominant.

The preoccupation with deviancy, as opposed to normalcy, encourages the
researcher to limit his scope and ignore some of the most vital elements of the
lives of the people he is studying. It has been noted by one sociologist that:

> It is probably a fact and one of which some contemporary students of deviance
> have peen cognizant—that the greater portion of the lives of deviant persons or
> groups is spent in normal, mundane, day-to-day living. In the researcher's focus
> on deviance and this acquisition of the deviant perspective, not only is he likely
> to overlook these more conventional phenomena, and thus become insensitive
> to them, but he may in the process overlook that very data which helps to ex-
> plain that deviance he studies.[3]

Having been equipped with the deviant perspective in my academic training, yet lacking strong commitment to it because it conflicted with my objective knowledge and responses to the Black women I was studying, I went into
the field equipped with a set of preconceived ideas and labels that I intended
to apply to these women. This, of course, meant that I had gone there only to
validate and elaborate on what was alleged to exist. If I had continued within
this context, I would have concluded the same thing that most social scientists who study Black people conclude: that they are pathology-ridden.

However, this role was difficult, if not impossible, for me to play because
all of my life experiences invalidated the deviant perspective. As I became
more involved with the subjects of this research, I knew that I would not be
able to play the role of the dispassionate scientist, whose major objective was
to extract certain data from them that would simply be used to describe and
theorize about their conditions. I began to perceive my role as a Black person,
with empathy and attachment, and, to a great extent, their day-to-day lives
and future destinies became intricately interwoven with my own. This did not
occur without a considerable amount of agonizing self-evaluation and conflict over "whose side I was on." On the one hand, I wanted to conduct a study
that would allow me to fulfill certain academic requirements, i.e., a doctoral

dissertation. On the other hand, I was highly influenced by my Blackness—by the fact that I, on many levels, was one of them and had to deal with their problems on a personal level. I was largely unable to resolve these strands, this "double consciousness," to which W. E. B. DuBois refers.[4] It is important to understand that Blacks are at a juncture in history that has been unprecedented for its necessity to grope with and clarify and define the status of our existence in American society. Thus, I was unable to resolve the dilemmas I faced as a Black social scientist because they only symbolized the larger questions, issues and dilemmas of our times.

Many books have been written about the Black community[5] but very few have really dealt with the intricate lives of the people who live there. By and large, they have attempted to analyze and describe the pathology which allegedly characterizes the lives of its inhabitants while at the same time making its residents responsible for its creation. The unhealthy conditions of the community such as drug addiction, poverty, crime, dilapidated housing, unemployment and the multitude of problems which characterize it have caused social analysts to see these conditions as producing millions of "sick" people, many of whom are given few chances ever to overcome the wretchedness which clouds their existence. Few authorities on the Black community have written about the vast amount of strength and adaptability of the people. They have ignored the fact that this community is a force which not only acts upon its residents but which is also acted upon. Black people are involved in a dynamic relationship with their physical and cultural environment in that they both influence and are influenced by it. This reciprocal relationship allows them to exercise a considerable amount of power over their environs. This also means that they are able to exercise control over their futures, whereas writers have tended to view the low-income Black community as an all-pervasive force which is so devastating as to compel its powerless residents to succumb to its pressures. Their power to cope and adapt to a set of unhealthy conditions—not as stereotyped sick people but as normal ones—is a factor which few people seem to accept or even realize. The ways Blacks have adapted to poverty and racism, and yet emerged relatively unscarred, are a peculiar quality which Americans should commend.

The concept of social deviance is quite frequently applied to the values and behavior of Blacks because they represent a departure from the traditional white middle-class norm, along with criminals, homosexuals and prostitutes.

But these middle-class standards should not have been imposed because of the distinctiveness that characterizes the Black life-style, particularly that of the masses.

Most scholars have taken a dim view of any set of distinct life-styles shared by Blacks, and where they were acknowledged to exist, have of course maintained that these forces were negative adaptations to the larger society. There has never been an admission that the Black community is a product of American social policy, not the cause of it—the structure of the American social system, through its practices of institutional racism, is designed to create the alleged "pathology" of the community, to perpetuate the "social disorganization" model of Black life. Recently, the Black culture thesis has been granted some legitimization as an explanatory variable for much of the distinctiveness of Black life. As a result of this more positive attitude toward understanding the strengths of life in the Black community, many scholars, policy makers et al. are refocusing their attention and reinterpreting the many aspects of life that comprise the complex existence of American Blacks.

There must be a strong concern with redefining the problem. Instead of future studies being conducted on problems of the Black community as represented by the deviant perspective, there must be a redefinition of the problem as being that of institutional racism. If the social system is viewed as the source of the deviant perspective, then future research must begin to analyze the nature of oppression and the mechanisms by which institutionalized form of subjugation are initiated and act to maintain the system intact. Thus, studies which have as their focal point the alleged deviant attitudes and behavior of Blacks are grounded within the racist assumptions and principles that only render Blacks open to further exploitation.

The challenge to social scientists for a redefinition of the basic problem has been raised in terms of the "colonial analogy." It has been argued that the relationship between the researcher and his subjects, by definition, resembles that of the oppressor and the oppressed, because it is the oppressor who defines the problem, the nature of the research and, to some extent, the quality of interaction between him and his subjects. This inability to understand and research the fundamental problem—neo-colonialism—prevents most social researchers from being able accurately to observe and analyze Black life and culture and the impact racism and oppression have upon Blacks. Their inability to understand the nature and effects of neo-colonialism in the same manner as Black people is rooted in the inherent bias of the social sciences. The basic concepts and tools of white Western society are permeated by this partiality to the conceptual framework of the oppressor. It is simple enough to say that the difference between the two groups—the oppressor and the oppressed—prevents the former from adequately comprehending the essence of Black life and culture because of a fundamental difference in perceptions, based upon separate histories, life-styles and purposes for being. Simply put, the slave and his master do not view and respond to the world in the same way. The historian Lerone Bennett addresses this problem below:

George Washington and George Washington's slaves lived different realities. And if we extend that insight to all the dimensions of white American history we will realize that blacks lived at a different time and a different reality in this country. And the terrifying implications of all this is that there is another time, another reality, another America. . .

Bennett states further that:

It is necessary for us to develop a new frame of reference which transcends the limits of white concepts. It is necessary for us to develop a total intellectual offensive against the false universality of white concepts whether they are expressed by William Styron or Daniel Patrick Moynihan. By and large, reality has been conceptualized in terms of the narrow point of view of the small minority of white men who live in Europe and North America. We must abandon the partial frame of reference of our oppressors and create new concepts which will release our reality, which is also the reality of the overwhelming majority of men and women on this globe. We must say to the white world that there are things in the world that are not dreamt of in your history and your sociology and your philosophy.[6]

Currently there are efforts underway to "de-colonize" social research on the conceptual and methodological levels.[7]

Although I attempted to maintain some degree of objectivity, I soon began to minimize and, very often, negate the importance of being "value-free," because the very selection of the topic itself reflected a bias, i.e., I studied Black women because of my strong interest in the subject.

I decided whose side I was on and resolved within myself that as a Black social scientist I must take a stand and that there could be no value-free sanctuary for me. The controversy over the question of values in social research is addressed by Gouldner:

If sociologists ought not express their personal values in the academic setting, how then are students to be safeguarded against the unwitting influence of these values which shape the sociologist's selection of problems, his preferences for certain hypotheses or conceptual schemes, and his neglect of others? For these are unavoidable and, in this sense, there is and can be no value-free sociology. The only choice is between an expression of one's values as open and honest as it can be, this side of the psychoanalytic couch, and a vain ritual of moral neutrality which, because it invites men to ignore the vulnerability of reason to bias, leaves it at the mercy of irrationality.[8]

I accepted this position as a guiding premise and proceeded to conduct my research with the full knowledge that I could not divorce myself from the problems of these women, nor should I become so engrossed in them that I would lose my original purpose for being in the community. The words of Kenneth

Oark, as he describes the tensions and conflicts he experienced while conducting the research for his classic study of Harlem, *Dark Ghetto*, typify the problems I faced:

> I could never be fully detached as a scholar or participant. More than forty years of my life had been lived in Harlem. I started school in Harlem public schools. I first learned about people, about love, about cruelty, about sacrifice, about cowardice, about courage, about bombast in Harlem. For many years before I returned as an "involved observer," Harlem had been my home. My family moved from house to house, and from neighborhood to neighborhood within the walls of the ghetto in a desperate attempt to escape its creeping blight. In a very real sense, therefore, *Dark Ghetto* is a summation of my personal and lifelong experiences and observations as a prisoner within the ghetto long before I was aware that I was really a prisoner.[9]

The inability to be objective about analyzing poverty, racism, disease, self-destruction and the gamut of problems which faced these females only mirrored a broader problem in social research. That is, to what extent should any scientist—white or Black—consider it his duty to be a dispassionate observer and not intervene, when possible, to ameliorate many of the destructive conditions he studies. On many occasions I found myself acting as a counselor, big sister, etc. Certainly the question can be raised as to whether researchers can continue to gather data on impoverished Black communities without addressing these findings to the area of social policy.

This raises another important question, to which I will address myself. That is, many people will read this book because they are seeking answers to the dilemmas and problems facing Black people in general and Black women in particular. A great number of young Black women will expect to find forever-sought formulas to give them a new sense of direction as Black Women. Some Black men will read this work because they are concerned about this new direction and want to become involved in the shaping of this process. Others, of course, will simply be curious to find out what a Black woman has to say about her peers. I expect traditional-type scholars to take great issue with my thesis and many of my formulations because I am consciously attempting to break away from the traditional way in which social science research has analyzed the attitudes and behavior patterns of Blacks. Finally, a small but growing group of scholars will find it refreshing to read a work on Black women which does nor indict them for all kinds of alleged social problems, which, if they exist, they did not create.

All of these are problems and questions which I view as inescapable for one who decides to attempt to break that new ground and write about areas of human life in ways in which they are not ordinarily approached.

There are no standard answers for these dilemmas I faced, for they are simply microcosms of the larger Black community. Therefore, this work is not attempting to resolve the problems of Black womanhood but to shed light on them. More than anything else, I feel that it is attempting to depict what the Black woman's life has been like in the past, and what barriers she has had to overcome in order to survive, and how she is coping today under the most strenuous circumstances. Thus, I am simply saying, "This is what the Black woman was, this is how she has been solving her problems, and these are ways in which she is seeking to alter her roles." I am not trying to chart a course of action for her to follow. This will, in large strenuous circumstances. Thus, I am simply saying, "This is what the Black woman was, this is how she has been solving her problems, and these are ways in which she is seeking to alter her roles." I am not trying to chart a course of action for her to follow. This will, in large measure, be dictated by, and interwoven with, the trends set in that vast Black American community. My primary concern here is with depicting the strength of the Black family and Black girls within the family structure. I will seek to depict the lives of Black people I knew who were utilizing their scant resources for survival purposes, but who on the whole were quite successful with making the necessary adaptive and creative responses to their oppressed circumstances. I am also dealing with the somewhat abstract white middle-class system of values as it affects Blacks. It is hoped that the problems I encountered with conducting such a study, as well as the positive approach I was eventually able to take toward this work, will enable others to be equally as effective in breaking away from an intellectual tradition which has existed far too long.

One of the primary preoccupations of every American adolescent girl, regardless of race and social class background, is that of eventually becoming a woman. Every girl looks forward to the time when she will discard the status of child and take on the role of adult, wife and possibly mother.

The official entry into womanhood is usually regarded as that time when she reaches the prescribed legal age (eighteen and sometimes twenty-one), when for the first time she is granted certain legal and other rights and privileges. These rights, such as being allowed to vote, to go to certain "for adults only" events, to join certain social clubs and to obtain certain types of employment, are accompanied by a type of informal understanding that very few privileges, either formal or informal, are to be denied her where age is the primary prerequisite for participation. Entry into womanhood is the point at which she is considered by older adults to be ready to join their ranks because she has gone through the necessary apprenticeship program—the period of adolescence. We can observe differences between racial and social class groups regarding, for instance, the time at which the female is considered to be ready to assume the duties and obligations of womanhood. Becoming a woman in the low-income Black community is somewhat different from the routes followed by the white middle-class girl. The poor Black girl reaches her Status of womanhood at an earlier age because of the different prescriptions and expectations of her culture. There is no single set of criteria for becoming a woman in the Black community; each girl is conditioned by a diversity of factors depending primarily upon her opportunities, role models, psychological disposition and the influence of the values, customs and traditions of the Black community. It will be demonstrated that the resources which adolescent girls have at their disposal, combined with the cultural heritage of their communities, are crucial factors in determining what kind of women they become. Structural and psychological variables are important as focal points because neither alone is sufficient to explain the many factors involved with psychosocial development. Therefore, the concepts of motivation, roles and role model, identity and socialization, as well as family income, education, kin and peer group relations are important to consider in the analysis. These diverse factors have rarely been considered as crucial to an analysis of Black womanhood. This situation exists because previous studies have substituted simplistic notions for rigorous multivariate analysis. Here, however, these multiple factors and influences will be analyzed as a "Black cultural" framework which has its own autonomous system of values, behavior, attitudes, sentiments and beliefs.

Another significant dimension to be considered will be the extent to which Black girls are influenced by the distinct culture of their community. Certain historical as well as contemporary variables are very important when describing the young Black woman. Her cultural heritage, I feel, has played a stronger role than has previously been stated by most writers in shaping her into the entity she has become.

Life in the Black community has been conditioned by poverty, discrimination and institutional subordination. It has also been shaped by African cultural survivals. From slavery until the present, many of the African cultural survivals influenced the way Blacks lived, responded to others and, in general, related to their environment. Even after slavery many of these survivals have remained and act to forge a distinct and viable set of cultural adaptive mechanisms because discrimination acted as an agent to perpetuate instead of to destroy the culture.

I will illustrate, through depicting the lives of Black preadolescent and adolescent girls in a big-city slum, how distinct sociohistorical forces have shaped a very positive and practical way of dealing and coping with the world. The values, attitudes, beliefs and behavior emerge from a long tradition, much of which has characterized the Black community from its earliest beginnings in this country.

What is life like in the urban Black community for the "average" girl? How does she define her roles, behaviors, and from whom does she acquire her models for fulfilling what is expected of her? Is there any significant disparity between the resources she has with which to accomplish her goals in life and the stated aspirations? Is the typical world of the teenager in American society shared by the Black girl or does she stand somewhat alone in much of her day-to-day existence?

In an attempt to answer these and other questions, I went to such a community and sought out teenagers whom I felt could provide me with some insights. I was a research assistant in 1964 on a study of an all-Black low-income housing project of over ten thousand residents in a slum area of St. Louis. (This study was supported by a grant from the National Institute of Mental Health, Grant No. MH-9189, "Social and Community Problems in Public Housing Areas.") It was geographically located near the downtown section of St. Louis, Missouri, and within one of the oldest slum areas of the city. The majority of the females were drawn from the Pruitt-Igoe housing project, although many resided outside the public housing project in substandard private housing.

At that time my curiosity was centered around the various activities in which the girls engaged that frequently produced harmful consequences. Specifically, I attempted to understand how such social problems as pregnancy, pre-marital sex, school dropout, etc. affected their life chances for success. I also felt, at the time, that a less destructible adaptation could be made to their impoverished environments. However, I was to understand later that perhaps a very healthy and successful adaptation, given their limited resources, had been made by all of these girls to a set of very unhealthy environmental conditions. Therefore, I soon changed my focus and attempted to apply a different perspective to the data.

I spent almost four years interviewing, testing (Thematic Apperception Test), observing and, in general, "hanging out" with these girls. I attempted to establish a strong rapport with all of them by spending a considerable amount of time in their homes with them and their families, at church, parties, dances, in the homes of their friends, shopping, at my apartment and in a variety of other situations. The sample consisted of several peer groups which over the years changed in number and composition. I always endeavored to interview their parents, and in some cases became close friends of their mothers. The field work carried me into the community at very unregulated hours — weekends, occasional evenings and during school hours (when

I usually talked to their mothers). Although a great portion of the data collected is exploratory in nature, the majority of it is based on systematic open-ended interviews that related to (1) life histories and (2) attitudes and behavior that reflected approaching womanhood. During the last year and a half I randomly selected thirty girls between the ages of thirteen and eighteen and conducted a systematic investigation that was designed to test many of my preliminary conclusions drawn from the exploratory research. All of the interviews and observations were taped and transcribed. The great majority of the interviews were taped live, and will appear as direct quotations throughout this book. (All of the girls have been given pseudonyms.)

I feel that the data are broad in scope and are applicable to almost any group of low-income Black teenage girls growing up in any American city. The economic, political, social and racial factors which have produced neo-colonialism on a national scale operate in Chicago, Roxbury, Detroit, Watts, Atlanta—and everywhere else.

The total misrepresentation of the Black community and the various myths which surround it can be seen in microcosm in the Black female adolescent. Her growing-up years reflect the basic quality and character environment, as well as anticipations for the future. Because she is in perhaps the most crucial stage of psychosocial development, one can capture these crucial forces—external and internal—which are acting upon her, which, more than any other impact, will shape her long adult role. Thus, by understanding the nature processes of her development, we can also comprehend the more intricate elements that characterize the day-to-day lives of the Black masses.

NOTES

From *The Death of White Sociology*. Joyce A. Ladner (ed). New York: Vintage Books, 1973, pp. 414–428. Reprinted by Permission.

1. Howard S. Becker, *The Outsiders*, New York, Free Press, 1963, p: 9.

2. See the works of Edwin Lemert, *Social Pathology*, New York, McGraw-Hill, 1951; John Kituse, "Societal Reaction to Deviance: Problems of Theory and Method," *Social Problems*, Winter 1962, pp,. 247–56; and Frank Tannenbaum, *Crime and the Community*, New York, Colombia University Press, 1938.

3. See Ethel Sawyer, "Methodological Problems in Studying Socially Deviant Communities," this volume.

4. W. E. B. DuBois, *Souls of Black Folk*, New York, Fawcett World Library, 1961.

5. I am using the term "Black community" to refer to what is traditionally called the "ghetto." I am speaking largely of the low-income and working-class masses, who comprise the majority of the Black population in this country.

6. Lerone Bennett, *The Challenge of Blackness* (Chicago: Johnson Publishing Co., 1972).

7. Refer to Robert Blauner, "Internal Colonialism and Ghetto Revolt," *Social Problems*, Vol. 16, No. 4, Spring 1969, pp. 393–408; and see Robert Blauner and David Wellman, "Toward the Decolomzation of Social Research," in this collection.

8. Alvin W. Gouldner, "Anti-Minotaur: The Myth of a Value-Free Sociology." *Social Problems*, Winter, 1962, pp. 199–213.

9. Kenneth Clark, *Dark Ghetto*, New York, Harper & Row, 1965, p. xv.

Appendix D

Rethinking the Concept of "Minority": A Task for Social Scientists and Practitioners

Doris Wilkinson

Although sociologists have articulated the components and scope of the "minority" concept, many of the characteristics are no longer germane. Originally those placed in the category were viewed as subordinate and as possessing cultural or physical qualities not approved or preferred by the larger population. There has been no systematic questioning of ingrained seductive words and value-based constructions like "minority." This brief critique offers an evaluation of the "minority" conceptions that is so pervasive in the social and behavioral sciences, the print and broadcast media, politics, and the entire language system.

INTRODUCTION

In current academic discourse, feminist theory and critiques of post-modem thinking have ushered in reappraisals of conventional language, especially about gender. However, this has not led to objective interpretations of how men and women of non-white racial and ethnic groups translate their experiences. Nor has there been any systematic questioning of ingrained seductive words and value-based constructions like minority. In the United States, at least, this latter notion represents a classic example of an ambiguous concept that is accepted as theoretically sound and scientifically measurable in the social sciences and given credibility in matters of policy. As an abstraction most often regarded as virtually synonymous with race, "minority" is actually non-scientific and devoid of conceptual clarity and empirical validity.

American Sociology has played a major role in generating a specialized vocabulary and in giving legitimacy to concepts like "minority." The field evolved from European philosophical roots as a social science permeated with values. Numerous biased terms and expressions like "invasion" and "visibility" comprised the original sociological frames of reference. The preoccupation in the United States with racial differences institutionalized the minority idea and resulted in the absence of historical explanations of causal social forces (e.g., slavery, discrimination). Consequently, existing sociological concepts and theoretically derived assumptions linked to "minority" are without historical or scientific merit. Actually, they have suppressed realistic and unbiased examinations of racial attitudes, beliefs, and ideologies.

Although sociologists have articulated the components and scope of the "minority" concept, many of the characteristics are no longer germane. Originally those placed in the category were viewed as subordinate and possessing cultural or physical qualities not approved or preferred by the larger population. The assertion was that minorities have a shared sense of group identity. Interestingly, this was overlooked as also being a feature of majority groups. The initial definitions emphasized being self-conscious and viewing themselves as "objects of collective discrimination" (Wirth, 1945: 347). In establishing the boundaries of the identity of the excluded, Wirth stated that they possess an inherited status. Without presenting the influences of divergent power relations, he and other sociologists thought of a minority as a group singled out from others for "differential and unequal treatment." This formulation included biology, culture, structural, and perceptual aspects. Several of the traits assigned to "minorities" covered all racial and ethnic groups and economic classes including the "power elite."

Basically, the label "minority" is engulfed in political connotations and refers to behaviors as well as biological traits. As a multidimensional and generic notion, it encompasses behavior but negates ethnicity and cultural distinctiveness. Additionally, this linguistic tool does not denote the vast contrasts that are characteristic of ethnic and racial group life. The variability embodied in ethnic traditions, lifestyles and group modes of affirming collective identity are not reflected in the assorted meanings of "minority" (Aguirre and Messineo, 1997; Snyder, 1990; Wright, 1997).

Moreover, "minority" does not accurately incorporate the histories and biographies of diverse ethnic and racial populations such as American Indian, Mexican American, African American, Puerto Rican, and Asian American (Feagin and Sikes, 1995; Garcia, 1997; Harjo, 1993; Mendoza, 1994; Snipp, 1989; Wilkinson, 1990). That is, the concept appears to have no relevance to ancestral linkages that provide a sense of family and community unity. An underlying thesis of this discussion is that social science interpretations of identities must be group-centered as well as racially specific. Ethnic affiliation and racial attachment, as opposed to externally ascribed "minority" status, are essential parallels with social placement and self-images (Plummer, 1995; Ramsey, 1991).

This brief critique offers an evaluation of the "minority" conception that is so pervasive in the social and behavioral sciences, the print and broadcast media, politics, and the entire language system. Given my long-term interest in the language that frames sociological theory and research, an insightful review of the concept in *Race, Gender & Class (Nibert*, 1996) was well received. While I have a different perspective on alternatives, the author correctly described "minority" as a "sociological euphemism." In the discussion, the evolution of the abstraction is interpreted with respect to the reasons for the sustained reliance on this particular term instead of "oppressed groups." The author states that "the term [constitutes] a social scientific euphemism for the victims of widespread exploitation, injustice and incalculable hardship and suffering . . ." Highlighting trends involving possible substitutions, aspects of the thesis offer a starting point for this discussion (Nibert, 1996: 131).

As this critical analysis will show, unlike other immigrant populations designated as minorities, African Americans have encountered a myriad of barriers since their forced arrival. Throughout the twentieth century, obstacles to upward mobility and equal life chances have confronted them. No other ethnic group in the United States has been enslaved or has faced perpetual racial segregation and discrimination in all institutional domains. Only the American Indian's history approximates this legacy, to some degree. Against this background, the reasons given for continuing the "minority" classification in the 21st century are overshadowed by historical forces. The expression simply does not enable understanding of the immense cultural and racial heterogeneity that typifies American society.

OBJECTIVES

Contextualized within the culture of the United States, two central questions guide this argument. (1) *What are some major deficiencies associated with the minority concept?* (2) *How can the minority idea be transformed and removed from the social science vocabulary?* Another important question guiding this inquiry is *what are the scientific and policy issues associated with the word minority?* At the outset, the basic principle is reaffirmed that identifying individuals by their race or ethnic background is no less important than recognizing them by their gender or sexuality. All of these indicators provide a sense of the essence of individuality and communal solidarity. Self-knowledge and feelings of personal worth are enhanced through articulating the components of one's identity. Learning is similarly advanced by becoming cognizant of the specific groups comprising the society.

An important related scientific and "sociology of knowledge" issue is why the word "minority" has been retained in the sciences and in the language system itself. While used in other countries where it most often refers to language minorities, in the United States the concept has always been ambiguous and value-laden. Since its origins, the word has been framed in negative imagery. Juxtaposed with problems of definition, typically those so labeled have been depicted as lacking in political and economic power. In addition, they have been considered as occupying the status of the culturally disadvantaged. Each of these descriptors carries a stigma (See: D'Amico, 1997; Goffman, 1963; Riggs, 1997; Snyder, 1990).

POLITICAL LANGUAGE IN THE SOCIAL SCIENCES

Science and the various professions have special modes of constructing and using language. Among the principal requirements in scientific reasoning is that concepts should be reliable, capable of measurement, and empirically verifiable. Correspondingly, clinical fields seek to rely on relatively precise diagnostic tools for behaviors and emotions. In spite of the particular paradigms in disciplines like sociology, innumerable words are obscure and without a reality basis. "Minority" is one of the key words that is imprecise.

The clarity and logic of concepts is a critical area in the social and behavioral sciences. While "minority" is applied incessantly, the category lacks concrete indicators and its miscellaneous attributes tend to be flawed and conflicting. Thus, given the wide variability among the diverse groups to whom the label refers, problems emerge with its application in social science paradigms. The difficulties disclosed with its usage are multiple. In fact, the contemporary qualities appear to confuse the initial definitions offered by sociologists.

Frequently, "minority" indicates only races (African Americans) or ethnic populations (Hispanics, Asians). At times, it extends to occupationally subordinated groups (e.g., women) and socially isolated populations. Multiracial (biracial persons) and economically depressed persons (unemployed, poor) are subsumed under the minority label. Sexual orientation, physical handicapped status and being white and male or female are similarly classified. It is also applied to processes and changes such as access to college, aging, migrants, opportunities, businesses, rights, issues in mental health, political perspectives ad infinitum.

Of special concern in this critical review is the use of the minority concept as representational and as an analytical medium. This interest stems from the interpretations and consequences of the word and its diversified nature as illustrated in the sciences and in the national media. Because "minority" does not meet any of the conventional standards for concept validity, it is an extremely problematic term in sociological inquiry. The numerous referents for the idea are not mutually exclusive. Thus, the array of meanings associated with it produce misleading conclusions. Ultimately, the complications surrounding minority have serious ramifications for social science generalizations as well as clinical practice.

THE MINORITY CHALLENGE

A few selected examples illuminate the contradictions inherent in the use of minority. In an instructive essay by William Raspberry, a perceptive and influential African American journalist, the mistake is made of using the word "minorities" to denote Blacks only, the group to whom he is referring. The author notes that "Black students at the College of Holy Cross [had] won the right to exclude whites from membership in the school-supported Black Student Union." The theme of the article is "In some instances, separation of the races helps minorities" (Raspberry, 1995: p. A9). However, the essay focuses solely on race.

Similarly, an article appeared in *Black Issues in Higher Education* on the challenges to private scholarships for minorities (Wright, 1997: 14–16). From the title, it was not clear whether the emphasis was on African Americans, sexual orientation, or handicapped status. Actually, the report focused on a student who felt that a community college in Northern Virginia violated the law by preventing Whites from applying for a particular scholarship. A mathematics instructor was quoted as saying that there "appears to be a major hysteria, or fear, of more minority students gaining access to colleges and universities" (Wright, 1997: 16). This comment is obviously not about females and gender issues nor sexual orientation. For, the single "minority" group presented is the African American.

Numerous studies have been designed to examine racial and ethnic bias in a variety of areas from housing and the occupational sphere to advertising. With respect to the latter, a Federal Communications Commission report on this subject appeared in *USA Today* (January 14, 1999). The findings revealed that "advertisers regularly discriminate against minority-owned radio stations and those that have large African American or Hispanic audiences" (Alexander, 1999).

Throughout the article, the word minority preceded the following: radio stations, listeners, consumers, media, hiring, and magazines. But, as one examines the results from the study by the Civil Rights Forum on Communications Policy, the consumer groups, stations, and audiences discussed are African American and Hispanic. In this context, minority was used as equivalent with race since the focus was on just two racial populations. Questioning such research as well as the presumption that minority is a useful classification provides a foundation for this discussion.

Finally, a *USA Today* report pertained to Denny's becoming one of the first advertisers to launch a campaign about race. The author stated that "with a high number of minority customers, Denny's can't ignore them" (Horovitz, 1999: 1B). Again, the primary "minority" being referred to is the African American. In most of the examples relating to African Americans, "minority" is used as a politically correct term to conceal racial specificity. As a matter of fact, the concept epitomizes one of the notable forms of politically correct language permeating sociology and the broader culture. The choice of this word marks the "sociological imagination" as well as the American national consciousness. Nibert (1996: 133) noted that "sociologists have been reluctant to call 'minority groups' oppressed because such a perspective is outside the range of accepted political discourse." Regardless, the term is not only deceptive in advertising but is inaccurate in the social sciences and inappropriate for policy decisions.

In earlier writings, I have used "minority" as a result of indoctrination in sociological reasoning and forced compliance with editorial stipulations (Wilkinson, 1980a, 1980b, 1987b). However, when I incorporated the term in an examination of psychotherapy, its coverage was clearly restricted.

> " . . . white therapists [must] be trained to understand the multicultural history of the society and to cope with racial and ethnic biases and race/sex role stereotypes, since these have an impact on the therapeutic experiences of minority women." (Wilkinson, 1980b: 297).

Selected issues encountered in psychotherapy with women from economically and educationally disadvantaged strata were explored. A significant void was observed in examinations of therapeutic processes and outcomes with "minority women (i.e., American Indian, Black or African American, Mexican American and Puerto Rican)" (Wilkinson, 1980b; 285). I pointed out that "most studies of racial and ethnic minorities had not been sex-specific." Nevertheless, my principal thesis at the time centered on African American women. Dissonance was evident throughout my usage of the term.

Again, in a demographic review of "Ethnicity" in the *Handbook of Marriage and the Family*, my hesitancy in using "minority" was obvious. In order to minimize misrepresentation, in the introduction I stated that:

"To date, most of the information on minority families had tended to mirror biases intrinsic in the nation's dominant culture. To counteract these biases an attempt has been made to incorporate the . . . conceptual frameworks . . . offered by contemporary minority scholars" (Wilkinson, 1987: 183).

"Minority families" were limited to those delineated by their racial heritage and ethnic lineage.

"Minority families differ from those in the majority population on the basis of race, ancestry, and other characteristics. They are part of a socially, politically, and economically subordinated population. Differential treatment is a significant consequence of minority status. The dominant minority groups (or populations) in the United States are Blacks or Afro-Americans, Chicanos or Mexican-Americans, Puerto Ricans, Japanese, Chinese, and Filipinos" (Wilkinson, 1987: 183).

As this discussion demonstrates, the word "minority" has substantial variation and hence translations. This invites illogical reasoning in its numerous applications. Groups so defined have very few shared attributes with respect to race, ethnicity, social class, gender, sexuality, and/or culture. In other words, minimal social and behavioral traits are held in common. Most groups detailed as minorities have separate class positions, racial and ethnic origins, family backgrounds, and life styles. Likewise, exposure to the opportunity structure and with oppression vary. Only one population assigned minority status in the Americas has ever been subjected to slavery and centuries of systemic racism (Darity, 1996; Dyson, 1997; Frankberg, 1993; Hooks, 1998; Hutchison, 1994; Levy, 1998; Reed, 1992; Wilkinson, 1987).

A MISSING DIMENSION: HISTORICAL PRECEDENTS

Dissecting the minority construction, a lack of understanding or even acceptance of macro-social forces and power differentials is evident with its use. Certainly, the impressionistic notion nullifies the effects of a post-slavery culture and the prevailing race-based and class hierarchy. Anchored within the matrix of economic inequality, the minority idea does not allow for the residual outcomes from race and class-related disparities. Using it to suggest sex/gender or behavior has an entirely different set of meanings and outcomes than applying the classification to ethnic and racial populations.

In most basic texts on race and ethnic relations, a "minority group" is defined as one that "has restricted power and an inferior status" or is "any group that has less than its proportionate share of wealth, power, and/or social status" (Farley, 1995: 7; Marger, 1991: 44–54). Size is usually not considered as the most important sociological factor. Thus, a minority group is one that

> "experiences a pattern of disadvantage or inequality, has a visible identifying trait, and is a self-conscious social unit. Membership is usually determined at birth and group members have a strong tendency to marry within the group" (Healey, 1995: 14).

Introducing the "visible trait or characteristic" that justifies mistreatment by the majority population, the above definition blends with "blaming the victim" assertions. Presumably, the traits may be of a variety of types ranging from cultural to physical or combinations of the two. Depending on the perspective, some groups are called ethnic minorities, while others are referred to as racial minorities. "The visibility factor" confirming membership in a particular racial or ethnic group has been explained as central to the minority thesis (Wirth, 1945). However, more recent interpretations maintain that minorities are determined not merely by race or ethnicity but by "sex, physical disability, lifestyle, or sexual orientation" (Farley, 1995: 7). Despite this, the historical and contemporary relationships between people of African and European descent are completely unlike those of any other groups so categorized.

Concentrating on visibility and embarrassed self-awareness does not permit grasping the pervasiveness of racial animosities and associated forms of prejudicial treatment. These are entirely separate social processes from the discrimination against groups because of their behaviors or physical limitations. Thus, the perplexing nature of "minority" is revealed in the virtually opposite groups included in its coverage.

In the final analysis, groups presented as minorities have faced vastly dissimilar patterns of acceptance and integration as well as exclusion and residential isolation. Further, intolerance and segregation have always been more injurious and permanent for African Americans than for any other ethnic Americans, regardless of social position or "visible" traits. Therefore, highlighting populations by their actual identities situates them within a narrative frame along with the dilemmas linked to the ethos of equal opportunity. With respect to the limited choices facing women of any ethnic or racial heritage, the minority conception calculatedly omits the intersection of class, gender and race (Wilkinson, 1997).

Probing the content of "minority" permits viewing it as depriving groups of their lived experiences. Its incongruous meanings have been created and reaffirmed by those who have not been among the economically, politically, and/or racially hindered populations. As pointed out earlier, the concept is devoid of historical specificity. Neither the aftereffects of American slavery on self identification nor the influence of the class system on economic status can be explained through its use. No provisions are made for interpreting the circumstances surrounding contemporary inequities that are repeated by other groups also classified as "minorities." Therefore, past and current disparities in opportunities and privileges are discounted through reliance on this impressionistic label. Since it is embedded in the political culture of the United States and hence in the social sciences, questions will be raised when confronting its idiosyncratic and ideological nature. Significant adjustments will be encountered by attempts to replace it since "minority" has been retained through custom and practice. Rationales will proliferate for preserving the concept in spite of the justifiable quest by groups to reclaim and define their own identities.

RECOMMENDATIONS FOR CHANGE

Researchers, clinicians, and teachers must seek ways to in-corporate race and ethnicity in all relevant contexts and omit entirely the "minority" concept. Since race is such a highly sensitive subject in the United States, a host of avoidance strategies restrict weighing its impact. On one hand, its influence is pervasiveness throughout American society and culture. On the other, the "minority" idea negates this reality. Fields that emphasize research and document identity issues must be among the first to reappraise the diffuse "minority" constellation.

Insisting on race and ethnic precision and race-consciousness is fundamental for addressing in a meaningful way economic and status disparities. The "minority" tag cannot yield solutions to issues bearing on racial injustices in the United States. Policies cannot be based on obscure ideas or presumed neutrality in the identification of groups in need. Specificity is imperative in policy formulation (Allen, Hunt and Gilbert, 1997; Culp, 1994; Reed, 1992; Rhode, 1997; Snyder, 1990; Wilkinson and King, 1987; Wright, 1997). With respect to this, in an examination of the Banneker scholarship program at the University of Maryland, researchers found that race-specificity remains necessary. This recommendation was made because of past, present and cumulative discrimination against African Americans (Allen, Hunt, and Gilbert, 1997). In other words, race-conscious policies in higher education are sound and necessary.

Scholars who explore language have described words as indicators of power and privilege. Ruling classes and majorities engage in identity dialogue that continually estranges existing disenfranchised and disadvantaged populations (Riggs, 1997). Thus, "minority" is substantively Eurocentric and reinforces erroneous racial assumptions. Along with its negative referents, the absence of commonalities among those so classified makes the word political and lacking in theoretical usefulness. Since "minority" is so deeply grounded in the American language system and psyche, as stated earlier, inevitably any change will become an arena of controversy.

Particularizing groups in the United States within the context of their racial and ethnic backgrounds is past due. No systematic evidence exists indicating that in this country, American Indians, Mexican Americans, Puerto Ricans, Asian and African Americans prefer assigning themselves a "minority" image or status. Rather, their orientation is toward the distinctiveness of their family lineage and the racial/ethnic groups to which they belong. In contrast to the vagueness of "minority group" (Nibert, 1996), the self-views of these populations have definitive historical and cultural meaning.

Additionally, the "minority" construction does not lead to any solutions for the numerous social problems correlated with economic levels and racial constraints in the United States. Rational policies cannot be designed using generic categories. Unless words like subordinated or interiorized are used, "minority" has no plausible substitutes. Specific group recognition is an imperative in research and in policy formulation. Race and ethnic specificity and race-consciousness are indispensable for addressing problems and major forms of inequality.

Various contemporary perspectives have suggested that traditional modes of thinking have been devoid of the capacity to address the needs and self actualization experiences of diverse populations. This indicates that the different ways that women and men translate their lives is identity related. "Minority" does not convey either personal identity nor historical continuity. In order to accurately incorporate the life stories of women and men of different ethnic backgrounds, interpretations of their uniqueness must be gender-centered as well as racially and ethnically grounded. "Minority" serves as an anachronistic political device that obliterates natural and contingent social distinctions.

The comments presented in this discussion have not been without forethought. Also, they are not presented for continuous argument but rather for self-reflection, learning and understanding. They should prove helpful to those in the social and behavioral sciences and to others who have reinforced illogical constructs. Considering the numerous incongruities in the "minority" concept, scientists and practitioners will have to dissect all applications and cease using it. As noted earlier, while I have regrettably used the word in my early writings, I have sought to discontinue this practice (Wilkinson, 1980a; 1987b; 1980b; 1992).

Currently, the "minority" image is so broad that it includes groups exposed to a whole range of majority beliefs and norms of exclusion. Some of the groups are members of the numerically and politically dominant population. Since science is the study of difference, classifying on the basis of race, ethnicity and economic class should be normative. Continued attempts to connect, at any level, disabilities, sexual orientation, race, ethnicity, economic position and gender under a vague symbol is prejudicial and unreasonable. Describing the experiences of African Americans as characteristic of those encountered by sexual, language or handicapped "minorities" minimizes the far-reaching impact of the country's race ideology.

CONCLUSION

Via the "minority concept, the social sciences are weakened in theoretical logic. For among the predominant problems of the modern era and hence in sociology are those relating to class, race, ethnicity, immigrant status, and gender. While all frame social placement and self-conceptions, race is the most challenging and complex. The "minority" idea reduces the scientific challenges associated with careful and objective study of race and racism (Dyson, 1997; Hochschild, 1996; Levy, 1998).

In addition to hindering understanding of the effects of past and present exclusionary processes on identity, the "minority" classification disregards group attachments and the legitimacy of difference. By maintaining this ideologically encumbered and politically correct word, those who embrace it in their teaching impede the imaginations of others. Ironically, the "minority" concept restricts and simultaneously politicizes the "sociological imagination."

The unremitting incorporation of "minority" in scholarly writings and social science language ushers in the need to include ethnic origins and race in scientific analysis. African Americans should be called by their racial heritage which they may decide is "Black," Afro-American, or African American. The purposive act of dismissing identity through the "minority" lens eliminates being informed of the ongoing purposive subordination of particular populations on the basis of their race or ethnic status.

Social and behavioral scientists and social workers are products of cultures and distinct populations. They must be able to deal objectively with race, ethnic group membership and racism. To do so, requires immediate abandonment of the "minority" theme. A rational alternative is needed to eliminate it from the scientific literature, the print media, and the national conversation. When confirming theoretical principles and attempting to facilitate understanding of group differences, taking into account race and ethnic ancestry is mandatory.

Nearing the end of the twentieth century, it is thus imperative that we begin to alter the language and our mind-sets regarding the manifest and latent implications of the minority misnomer. Perhaps, one way to begin is to delineate possible options. The first involves deleting "minority" from the social and behavioral sciences because of its intrinsic biases, lessening of the significance of racialized economic inequality, and elimination of personal preferences. This step alone could improve the scientific credibility of selected disciplines. Retaining obscure and controversial language at the outset of the present century poses an especially compelling paradox for sociology.

The accent on minority standing overrides the necessity for bringing race and racism into research as well as into clinical therapy and social work practice. Dismissing race, ethnic identity, class status, and even gender through repeated use of the "minority" label reduces the ability to understand the authenticity of the life stories of distinct populations. The narratives of those so named are actually eradicated.

Considering gender, the "visibility" component of "minority" is offensive and unsuitable in the social sciences and in other fields. This feature does not contribute toward explaining outcomes bearing on the lives of women of Spanish, Asian, African and American Indian origin, for example. It is chronically misleading and undermines any appreciation of the personal stories of these racial/ethnic women. Recognizing the special identities that they have is much more principled than analyzing them using nebulous symbolism. The internalization of gender roles and ethnic and racial "being" is a central part of the self-definition process for women (Beale, 1970; Garcia, 1997; Morgan, 1993; St. Jean and Feagin, 1998; Wilkinson, 1995).

To reiterate, examinations of racial obstacles are clouded via the use of the term "minority." The word conceals the realities of particular group circumstances. Comparisons among those so typed erase the differential economic and political inferiorization of one population over another. Given this, the most important recommendation from this critique is that the concept must be instantly dismantled and constructive possibilities introduced that specify individual and collective identities. Ethnic and racial consciousness is a rational choice.

Overall, racial and ethnic specificity could have several positive outcomes: (1) accepting a population's authentic request to be defined and related to in terms of ancestry or other preferred status qualities, (2) facilitating sensible communication and meaningful interaction between the self and others, (3) providing a sense of in-group solidarity for those now portrayed as minorities, (4) enhancing knowledge of American history and the country's rich cultural diversity. These possibilities reinforce the recommendation that the exclusionary motif embodied in the notion of "minority" must be eradicated from social theory, research, and all policy decisions.

In the United States, race, class and ethnicity have been the principal molders of group interaction, work roles, power, and social hierarchy. Historical forces and change have dramatically shaped family life and occupational outcomes. The "minority" idea does not grasp these realities. Greater explicitness in setting priorities can be forthcoming with the deletion of the concept from the social sciences. Expectedly, any move toward change of this linguistic symbol will be an area of dispute and rationalization for its continuation. This is due to the fact that the word is entrenched in the broader cultural mores. Nevertheless, it must be recognized that the "minority" idea does not reflect America's racial and ethnic mixture.

Ultimately, the minority marker is not pertinent for dissecting the roots of racial inequality in the employment sector nor biases in the workplace. The term does not account for the stratification in employment nor contrasting occupational advantages among persons within the "minority" category some of whom are labeled on the basis of lifestyles. Several groups in the category have greater opportunities for upward mobility than others. That is, for selected populations judged as comparable, systemic differences in chances for success prevail. Thus, intermingling handicapped status, health conditions, and behaviors with race and ethnic heritage is problematic, unwarranted, and unfair to heretofore disenfranchised racial and ethnic populations.

Pretending that U.S. society . . . has moved beyond racial and gender biases to meritocracy ignores its long and continuing history of bias and inequality" (Rhode, 1997).

As interpreted in this critical assessment, "minority" is not an appropriate formation. Members of particular ethnic populations do not automatically describe themselves using this figure of speech. In contrast, those so defined by the dominant sector seek to have their stories, encounters, and needs included in analyses of their experiences. Their family and ancestral sagas are important to them. Removing "minority" from the lexicon of the social and behavioral sciences means that clarification in establishing hierarchies of need and sound public policy will be forthcoming.

NOTES

Journal of Sociology and Social Welfare, March, 2000, Volume XXVII, Number 1. Reprinted by Permission.

REFERENCES

Aguirre, A., & Messineo, M. (1997). Racially motivated incidents in higher education: What do they say about the campus climate for minority students? *Equity and Excellence in Education, 30,* 26–30.

Alexander, K. (1999, January 14). Communications study finds ad bias. *USA Today,* p. B7.

Allen, W., Hunt, D. M., & Gilbert, D. L (1997). Race-conscious academic policy in higher education: The University of Maryland Banneker Scholarship Program. *Educational Policy, 11,* 443–478.

Beale, F. (1970). Double jeopardy: To be black and female. In a T. Cade (Ed.), *The black woman: An anthology* (pp. 90–100). New York: New American Library.

Culp, J. M. (1994). Colorblind remedies and the intersectionality of oppression: Policy arguments masquerading as moral claims. *New York University Law Review, 69,* 162–195.

Darity, W. (1996). The undersirables, America's underclass in the managerial age: Beyond the Myrdal Theory of Racial Inequality. In a O. Clayton (Ed.) *An American dilemma revisited: Race relations in a changing world.* (pp. 112–137). New York: Russell Sage Foundation.

D'Amico, R. (1997). The continuing significance of race in minority male joblessness. In N. BaNikongo (ed.), *Leading issues in African American studies* (pp. 481–500). Durham, North Carolina: Carolina Academic Press.

Dyson, M. (1997). In a color-blind society, we can only see black and white: Why race will continue to rule. In M. Dyson, *Race rules: Navigating the color line* (pp. 213–224). New York: Random House/Vintage edition.

Farley, J. E. (1995). *Majority and minority relations* (3rd ed.). New Jersey: Prentice-Hall.

Feagin, J., & Sikes, M. (1995). How black students cope with racism on white campuses. *Journal of Blacks in Higher Education, 8,* 91–97.

Frankberg, R. (1993). *The social construction of whiteness: White women, race matters.* Minneapolis: University of Minnesota Press.

Garcia, A (1997). *Chicana feminist thought: The basic historical writings.* New York: Routledge.

Goffman, E. (1963). *Stigma: Notes on the management of a spoiled identity.* Englewood Cliffs, New Jersey: Prentice-Hall, Inc.

Harjo, S. (1993). The American Indian experience. In H. McAdoo (ed.), *Family ethnicity: strength in diversity* (pp. 199–207). California: SAGE.

Healey, J. F. (1995). *Race, ethnicity, gender and class.* Thousand Oaks, California: Pine Forge Press.

Hochschild, J. (1996). When books on race don't help us know the truth. *Journal of Blacks in Higher Education, 12,* 69–73.

Hooks, Bell. (1998). White oppression is to blame for black inequality. *In Inequality: Opposing viewpoints in social problems* (pp. 166–174). San Diego, California: Greenhaven Press, Inc.

Horovitz, B. (1999, January 12). Denny's airs anti-racism ads. *USA TODAY*. pp. IB.

Hutchison, E. O. (1994). *The assassination of the black male*. Los Angeles, California: Middle Passage Press.

Levy, P. (1998). The persistence of the color line. *Journal of Urban History, 24*, 235–243.

Mendoza, J. (1994). On being a Mexican American. *Phi Delta Kappan* 76 (December): 93–95.

Morgan, J. (1993). Professor studies 'Those loud black girls'. *Black Issues in Higher Education*, (June 3), 20–21.

Nibert, D. (1996). Note on minority group as sociological euphemism. *Race, Gender & Class, 3*, 129–136.

Plummer, D. L. (1995). Patterns of racial identity development of African American adolescent males and females. *Journal of Black Psychology, 21*, 168–180.

Ramsey, P. (1991). The salience of race in young children growing up in an all-white community. *Journal of Educational Psychology, 83*, 28–34.

Raspberry, W. (1995, November 24). In some instances, separation of the races helps minorities. *Lexington Herald Leader*, p. A9.

Reed, W. (1992). Black men and their families: Issues and options. *Challenge: A journal of research on African American men, 3*, 28–38.

Rhode, D. L. (1997). Affirmative action. *National Forum*, 77, 12–16.

Riggs, S. H. (1997). The rhetoric of othering. In S.H. Riggins *The language and politics of exclusion: Others in discourse*, pp. 1–30. California: SAGE.

Snipp, C. M. (1989). *American Indians: The First of this Land*. New York: Russell Sage Foundation.

Snyder, H. N. (1990). *Growth in Minority detentions attributed to drug law violations*. Washington, D.C.: U.S. Department of Justice, Office of Juvenile Justice and Delinquency Prevention.

St. Jean, Y. and J. Feagin. (1998). *Double Burden: Black Women and Everyday Racism*. New York: M. E. Sharpe, Inc.

Wilkinson, D. (l980a). "A Profile: Minorities in Sociology and Other Behavioral Sciences." *ASA Footnotes* (Official Newsletter of the American Sociological Association 6 (November): 6–8.

———.(1990). "Americans of African Identity." *Society, 27*, (May-June); 14–18.

———.(1987b). "Ethnicity." Pp. 183–210 in M. Sussman and S. Steinmetz (eds.). *Handbook of Marriage and the Family*. New York: Plenum Press.

———.(1995). "Gender and Social Inequality: The Prevailing Significance of Race." *Daedalus 124*; 167–178.

———.(1980b). "Minority Women; Social-Cultural Issues." In A. Brodsky and R. Hare-Mustin (eds.). *Women and Psychotherapy: An Assessment of Research and Practice*. (pp. 285–304). New York: Guilford Press.

———.(1992). "Minorities and Women in the Liberation of the ASA, 1964–1974." *The American Sociologist, 23*, (Spring); 7–10.

———.((1997). "Reappraising the Race, Class, Gender Equation: A Critical Theoretical Perspective." *Smith College Studies in Social Work, 67*, (June): 261–276.

Wilkinson, D. and G. King. (1987). "Conceptual and Methodological Issues in the Use of Race as a Variable: Policy Implications." *The Milbank Quarterly, 5*, 56–71.

Wirth, L. (1945). "The Problem of Minority Groups." In R. Linton (ed.). *The Science of Man in the World Crisis.* New York: Columbia University.

Wright, S. (1997). "Private Scholarships for Minorities Challenged." *Black Issues in Higher Education, 14*, 14–16.

African American Women since the Second World War: Perspectives on Gender and Race

Delores P. Aldridge

African American women have sought many things, among them an authentic paradigm that could explain their lives and act as a template for their becoming all they are capable of being. The focus, then, of this chapter is on the various concepts and perspectives that have been presented to provide an understanding of what has meaning and importance to black women as they have sought fulfilling lives since the Second World War. Could African American women fit into a women's or the feminist movement the originally scorned traditional female roles—ones which were prompted as ideal not only in white society, but in black society as well? How did black females view the: Women's Movement in the 1960s and 1970s, a movement led by a group which heretofore had subjugated and humiliated them? Is feminism interchangeable with black feminism, or womanism, or Africana womanism? What are the values of contemporary feminism and what is the African American woman's fit in contemporary feminism? Is the new or contemporary feminism the key to black women's agency and will it serve to form a union among all women and not just among white women? Where will black women put their priorities? In other words, do they see their future more with the black male or the white female? How will black women's priorities impact on the African American family and community? These are among the questions this chapter seeks to answer.

African American women have shared various perspectives on the concept and development of feminism and feminist theory, both of which became the subject of much discussion in the 1970s with the emergence of the Afriana/Black Studies Movement and the Feminist/Women Studies Movement. Many African American women were slow to embrace the terminology, while a minority became very active in identifying with a feminist movement. In order to effectively understand the dynamics of the Africana and Feminist movements one must consider not only changes in individuals, but cultural changes as well. A social movement is not just a mass of individuals, but an ongoing social process. In relation to social change, the African American woman is also part of American society. Her propensity to embrace or reject a social movement led and controlled by white women, such as the feminist movement, has thus been partly a function of what her society has made of her and she of it.

BLACK WOMEN AND THEIR VIEWS ON THE WOMEN'S MOVEMENT/FEMINISM

Willa Hemmons, writing on the Women's Movement, noted:

> One cannot say that Black women will have positive attitude or negative attitudes toward the movement without specifying the characteristics of the woman. We found that Black women who were committed to the Black liberation movement were also committed to the women's liberation movement. Further, Black women who took traditional roles of women were less likely to embrace the ideas and values of the women's movement. Surprisingly, Black women were more "feminine" in their values than white women, but this did not decrease the percentage of women who showed a positive attitude toward the women's liberation movement. We have suggested that this inconsistency may result from the various non-tradition roles that Black women have played. In short, it is a result of Black women having a different history than white women. (Hemmons 1980: 296)

Hemmons goes on to say that

> Many Black women say they are unconcerned with giving up feminine behavior; they still want men to open doors for them and take them to dinner. At the same time, these women do not mind washing dishes, cooking, and taking care of children. What they want is the same economic benefits enjoyed by the white man. Black women do not want to invade all-male clubs because they do not want men to invade their clubs. Black women enjoy the sisterhood of other women; it is a part of their culture. Black women say they want the same education and job opportunities of white males. (ibid: 296)

Finally, Hemmons posits that the primary reason for black women's failure to join the Women's Movement was grounded in the priorities of the movement. When white women were into consciousness-raising sessions, trying to come to grips with who they were apart from their husbands and children, black women were seeking ways to address unemployment and unemployment among black people in general and black women in particular. When white women were trying to find time to write or do research, black women were searching for organizations and groups that would address the quality of education their children were receiving. When white women were crafting strategies for moving into the labor market and out of the house, large numbers of black women were suggesting that they would gladly return home and take care of their families if the economic system were not so oppressive for black men. At the same time, black women were saying to black men that to be in the home would not make them become subservient to black men (Hemmons 1980: 297). Data from Hemmon's study show that black women were indeed aware of their status as women. However, major issues for black women were not being addressed by the Women's Movement—issues of economic and racial oppression, issue that involved her men and her children, the very centrality of her existence.

A black Feminist Statement by The Combahee River Collective provides another perspective on black women, the Women's Movement, and feminism. In a statement dated April 1977, it raises the issues of difference among women and their perception of their relationship to the Women's Movement:

> We are a collective of black feminists who have been meeting together since 1974. During that time we have been involved in the process of defining and clarifying our politics, while at the same time doing political work within our own group and in coalition with other progressive organizations and movements. The most general statement of our politics at the present time would be that we are actively committed in struggling against racial, sexual, heterosexual, and class oppression and see as our particular task the development of integrated analysis and practice based upon the fact that the major systems of oppression are interlocking. The synthesis of these oppressions creates the conditions of our lives. As black women we see black feminism as the logical political movement to combat the manifold and simultaneous oppressions that all women of color face. . . . Although we are feminists and lesbians, we feel solidarity with progressive black men and do not advocate the fractionalization that white women who are separatists demand. Our situation as black necessitates that we have solidarity around the fact of race, which white women of course do not need to have with white men, unless it is their negative solidarity as racial oppressors. We struggle together with black men against racism, while we also struggle with black men about sexism. (Combahee River Collective 1977: 13)

They then link Feminism and the Black Movement with their political and economic positions:

> We realize that the liberation of all oppressed people necessitates the destruction of the political-economic systems of capitalism and imperialism as well as patriarchy.

We are socialists because we believe the work must be organized for the collective benefit of those who do the work and create the products and not for the profit of the bosses. Material resources must be equally distributed among those who create these resources. (ibid: 14)

It is clear the women of The Combahee River Collective understood the interrelationship between race, class, and gender. But not only did they articulate theory in identifying issues particularly relevant to black women, they were also involved in organizing and actively working toward elimination of inequity with the inclusiveness of their politics. Issues and projects that collectives members actually worked on included workplace organizing at a factory, sterilization abuse, abortion rights, battered women, rape, and health care. One issue of major concern that they addressed was racism in the white women's movement:

As black feminists we are made painfully aware of how little effort white women have made to understand and combat their racism, which requires among other things that they have a more than superficial comprehension of race, color, and black history and culture. Eliminating racism in the white women's movement is by definition work for white women to do, but we will continue to speak to and demand accountability on this issue. (Combahee River Collective 1977: 15)

In *All the Women Are White, All the Blacks Are Men, But Some of Us Are Brave*, three Africana women scholars wrote:

Women's Studies focused almost exclusively upon the lives of white women. Black Studies, which was much too often male-dominated, also ignored Black women . . . Because of white women's racism and Black men's sexism there was no room in either area for a serious consideration of the lives of Black women. And even when they have considered Black women, white women usually have not had the capacity to analyze racial politics and Black culture, and Black men have remained blind or resistant to the implication of sexual politics in Black women's lives. (Hull, Scott, Smith 1982: xx-xxi)

Clenora Hudson-Weems says that the emergence of black feminism in the 1970s, an offshoot of white feminism, has witnessed the response of many black women who have not readily embraced the concept of feminism for a variety of reasons, in spite of its legitimacy in the academy and the desire of many to be a legitimate part of the academic community. To be sure, embracing an established, acceptable theoretical methodology—feminism—is one of the most reliable, strategic means of ensuring membership into the powerful, visible community of academic women, which extends far beyond itself and secures for its supporters not only job possibilities and publications but also prestige and high visibility. While many other black women naively adopted feminism early on, because of the absence of an alternative and suitable framework for their individual needs as Africana women, more are reassessing the historical realities and the agenda for the modern feminist movement, and have barely stood firm in their outright rejection of it (Hudson-Weems 2000; 205).

Hudson-Weems strongly resists labeling all black women activists as feminists. According to her, while feminism—an agenda designed to meet the needs and demands of white women—is quite plausible for that group, placing all women's history under white women's history, thereby giving the latter the definitive position, is problematic. In fact, it demonstrates the ultimate of racist arrogance and domination, suggesting that authentic activity of women resides with white women. It is, therefore, ludicrous to claim as feminists such Africana women activists as Maria W. Steward and Frances Watkins Harper, abolitionist Sojourner Truth, militant abolition spokesperson and universal suffragist; Harriet Tubman, Underground Railroad conductor, Ida B. Wells, early twentieth century anti-lynching crusader; and Anna Julia Cooper, who proclaims in *A Voice from the South* that "Woman's cause is man's cause: [we] rise or stink together, dwarfed or godlike, bond or free" (ibid: 209).

In fact, black women got there first, long before feminists:

In considering the race-based activities of these early Africana women and countless other unsung Africana heroines, what white feminists have done in reality was to take the lifestyle and techniques of Africana women activists and use them as blueprints for framing their theory. They then proceed to name, define, and legitimize it as the only substantive women's movement. Thus, in defining the feminist and her activity, they are identifying with independent African women, women whom they both emulated and envied. (Hudson-Weems 2000: 210)

Bettina Aptheker, a white feminist herself, even sees the feminist priority as unworkable for the black woman:

When we place women at the center of our thinking, we are going about the business of creating a historical and cultural matrix from which women may claim autonomy and independence over their own lives. For women of color, such autonomy cannot be achieved in conditions of racial oppression and cultural genocide. In short, "feminism," in the modern sense, means the empowerment of women. For women of color, such an equality, such an empowerment, cannot take place unless the communities in which they live can successfully establish their own racial and cultural integrity. (Aptheker 1981: 13)

She recognizes the importance of prioritizing the race factor for the black woman as a prerequisite for dealing with the question of gender. This is not to say that gender issues are not important: they are real concerns for all women, black women included, as we are yet operating within a patriarchal system and therefore must confront this issue head on.

However, attacking gender biases does not translate into mandating one's identification with or dependency upon feminism as the only viable means of addressing them. Feminists have no exclusivity on gender issues. According to Vivian Gordon—in her book *Black Women, Feminism, and Black Liberation: Which way?*—

> To address women's issues, therefore, is not only to address the crucial needs of black women, it is also to address the historic primacy of the African and African American community; that is the primacy of its children and their preparation for the responsibilities and privileges of mature personhood. (Gordon 1991: viii)

Gordon's approach in dealing with women's issues is to bring out the historical reality of Africana people and the centrality of family for the security of future generations. Aldridge takes this a step further in her *Focusing: Black Male-Female Relations*, contending that derailing our race-based struggled for a gender-based one poses serious consequences:

> One might argue . . .that the women's liberation movement—as it is presently defined and implemented—has a negative impact on the Black Liberation movement . . . [for] Women's liberation operates within the capitalist tradition and accepts the end goals of sexist white males. (Aldridge 1991: 35)

Clearly, Aldridge understands well the perspective from which the feminist comes. In "Cultural and agenda in academia," Hudson-Weems succinctly puts it as "mainstream feminism is women's co-opting themselves into mainstream patriarchal values" (Hudson-Weems 1989: 187). The key issues for Hudson-Weems, Aptheker, Gordon, and Aldridge—three of them black and one white—is not the exclusion of gender issues, but rather the manner in which they are addressed.

From the perspectives emerging—from Hemmon's empirical study of African American women's attitudes toward the Women's Movement and feminism, and the self-defined black feminists of The Combahee River Collective, as well as from theorists Aptheker, Aldridge, Gordon, and Hudson-Weems—there exists strong positions about black women's fit in a racist, white-women-led movement or one defined as feminist. The Women's or Feminist Movement in the first several decades of existence was perceived as not embracing black women's major concern of the intersection of race, class, and gender.

The women whose views were analyzed by Hemmons (1980), The Combahee River Collective, and other women critics are not unlike outspoken African American women Intellectuals before them, who viewed the struggles of women of African descent in America as part of a wider struggle for human dignity and empowerment. As early as 1893, Anna Julia Cooper in a speech to women provided this perspective:

> We take our stand on the solidarity of humanity, the oneness of life and the unnaturalness and injustice of all special favoritisms, whether of sex, race, country, or condition . . . The colored woman feels that woman's cause is one and universal; and that not till race, color, sex, and condition are seen as accidents, and not the substance of life, not till the universal title of humanity to life, liberty, and the pursuit of happiness is conceded to be inalienable to all, not till then is woman's lesson taught and woman's cause won—not the white woman's not the black woman's, not the red woman's, but the cause of every man and of every woman who has writhed silently under a mighty wrong. (quoted in Loewenberg and Bogin 1976: 235)

The perspectives addressed above speak to the lives of African American women. And, some focus directly on concepts or terms in an effort to give clarity in defining black womanhood. However, it is important to move further into a discussion of some of the various terms and/or paradigms used in naming and defining black women's lives.

Feminism, Black Feminism, Womanism, Africana Womanism -The Same or Different?

The terms feminism, black feminism, womanism, and Aficana womanism—as explainers of the realities of black women's lives—have been proposed and defined by numerous critics and scholars. Some use one term giving it the meaning that someone else attributes to another term. Thus, some confusion exists about what is meant when the terms are used. Smith explains:

> Feminism is the political theory and practice that struggles to free all women: women of color, working-class women, poor women, disabled women, lesbians, old women—as well as white, economically privileged, heterosexual women. Anything less man this vision at total freedom is not feminism, but merely female self-aggrandizement. (Smith 1982: 49)

If this definition is to be accepted, then it must be conceded that feminism does not exist, as it has not embraced in theory or practice all women. According to Vivian Gordon,

Africana women were to elect to do so, they could lay an unprecedented historic claim to the lexicon "feminist" by simply citing the conditions over which they have struggled in the Americas, such as: (1) the right to control one's own reproduction; (2) freedom from sexual harassment; (3) equality before the law; (4) the right to vote; (5) equal pay for equal work (or historically, pay for work); (6) equal opportunity for a quality education; (7) quality housing; (8) quality health care, including preventive and rehabilitation services; (9) survivors' benefits for families; (10) old age security; (11) nonpunitive assistance programs for the qualified poor; and (12) the abolition of racism and sexism in the criminal justice system. (Gordon 2000: 166)

Gordon stresses that

> their rebellion during the enslavement; their devotion to family; their copartnership with men in the fight against oppression; their demonstrated ability to do work, including "traditional man's work;" their historic organization, which demonstrates an ability to organize on behalf of the elevation of positions of women; their involvement in the development of educational and business institutions. As well as their contributions to science, medicine, and technology from the times of the ancients to the present; more than qualifiy Africana women as the first "feminists." That they have continuously elected to not compartmentalize their identity into categories of race versus gender bars further discussion. (Gordon 2000: 166)

Gordon continues:

> The lexicon of feminism is conceptually exclusive. It is seated in a gender-specific identity, which is a female response to the unique experiences of a male supremacy that America is justified by a culturally rooted belief system that traces back to a Greco-Roman legacy. African American women linked to their ancestral past grounded in collective consciousness are guided by their identification with the total community—which is ultimately the extended kin, as opposed to an ongoing isolated gender-specific identity. (ibid: 167)

In African cosmology, proper naming—*nommo*—says it all, as it is essential to existence, which makes it all the more difficult to accept an improper name for oneself. In 1983, Alice Walker identified with the term womanist, of which she says "womanist is to feminist as purple is to lavender," addressing the notion of the solidarity of humanity. She defines "womanist" in her book *In Search of Our Mothers' Gardens: Womanist Prose*. For Walker, a "womanist" is one who is "committed to the survival and wholeness of an entire people."

Clenora Hudson-Weems (1993) provides us with another concept that differs subtly from womanism—Africana womanism. The Africana refers not only to continental Africans, but also to people of African descent worldwide.

The concept, Africana, perhaps first received national visibility as a descriptor of Africana Studies with the naming of the Africana Studies and Research Center at Cornell University. In the book, *Africana Womanism: Reclaiming Ourselves*, Hudson-Weems explores the dynamics of the conflict between the mainstream feminist, the black feminist, womanism and the Africana womanist. In this work, she sets forth 18 principles in the African womanism paradigm. Among these are self-naming, self-defining, family centered, and cooperative male-female relationships.

According to Hudson-Weems, Africana womanism is neither an outgrowth nor an addendum to mainstream feminism, but rather a concept grounded in the culture of—and which focuses on the experiences, needs, and desires of—Africana women. Africana womanists and feminists have separate agendas. Feminism is female centered; Africana womanism is family centered. Feminism is concerned primarily with ridding society of sexism; Africana womanism is concerned with ridding society of racism first, then classism, and sexism. Many feminists say their number one enemy is the male; Africana womanists welcome and encourage male participation in their struggle. Feminism, Hudson-Weems says, is incompatible with Africana women, as it was designed to meet the needs of white women.

Black feminism is a paradigm designed to bring black women into the told of white feminism. These new black feminists now emphasize race, as well as gender and class, as critical to understanding the lives of black women—an orientation long shared by many other black women who did not identify with feminism. Those black women who continue to use the term feminism as a theoretical construct for their analysis receive considerable support for their research. Aligning themselves with the framework of feminism has proved to be a relevant strategy for acceptance into that established community—a membership which carries many benefits, such as visibility, numerous employment possibilities, and publications. Such a reward system cannot be dismissed or minimized, because it is highly influential on black feminists and their allegiance to, and identification with, dominant feminist ideologies. Often these same feminists, under the guise of a "new feminism," have duplicated work and/or misappropriated practical and theoretical constructs of scholars and critics who have stressed race, gender, and class, with a focus on the family and community survival of black people.

NEW BLACK FEMINISM

Contemporary scholars, black and non-black, who write on women's lives concede that the development of an intersectional perspective on gender and race is rooted in the work of scholars studying women of color. Several prominent black female historians have focused on the frustration and triumph of black women who have been faced with the double burden of race and sex (Brown 1989; Rouse 1989; Shaw 1996). This body of work on gender and race is usually referred to under the rubric of multiracial feminism, multicultural feminism, or postcolonial feminism (Zinn and Dill 1996; Lorber 1998; Mohanty 1991). As part of this endeavor, contemporary or new feminist theory has become pivotal in proposing treatment that is inclusive of race and gender in determining labor market outcomes (Brewer 1993; Collins 1999; James and Busia 1993). Relying on an experience-based epistemology, black women revealeed that not only were both race and gender implicated in shaping their lives, but neither the extant theories of gender as "simultaneous and linked" social identities or race as paramount or sufficient to explain their lives, rather "both and . . . was necessary (Cade 1970; Brewer 1993; Glenn 1999; Hooks 1989; Hull et al. 1982; Spelman 1988).

Sara Evans (1979) wrote one of the first books to underscore the invaluable role of women in the Civil Rights Movement. *Personal Politics: The Roots of Women's Liberation in the Civil Rights Movement and the New Left* was a triumph in establishing black women as role models in organizing young white women workers from the South and the North. Interestingly, however, white women borrowing from black women became the definers and leaders of the Women's Movement. And while black women historians contend that scholars on the South's white women and black women have found common ground, other black women scholars differ (Crawford, Rouse and Woods 1999). For example, both Gordon (2000) and Hudson-Weems (2000), who identify with Africana womanism, have insisted on the importance of naming and defining one's paradigms to provide understanding of and direction for the lives of black women, their families, and communities. Both insist the proper naming of a thing will in turn give it essence. They, as does Toni Morrison in *Beloved*, maintain: "Definitions belong to the definers not the defined. Self naming and self defining is crucial" (Morrison 1987).

On the other hand, Collins—in "What's in a name . . . ?"—asserts:

> Rather than developing definitions and arguing over naming Practices—for example, whether this thought should be called Black feminism, womanism, Afrocentric Feminism, Africana womanism, and the like—a more useful approach lies in revisiting the reasons why black feminist thought exists at all. (Collins 1996: 22)

Clearly, from this quotation, she is not in agreement with Gordon, Hudson-Weems, and Morrison. Obviously she does not embrace the concept of *nommo*, or she would not have ended by proposing such a question. More importantly, why does Collins retain the term "feminist," rejecting a more authentic one? This is the dilemma within which black feminism finds itself. Holding on to a term but yet incorporating facets of a paradigm or paradigms that they have not acknowledged as more authentic for black women, indeed black people. They have too often camouflaged their so-called "new black feminism," as introduced by Hortense Spillers at the 2000 Du Bois Conference in Philadelphia. The new black feminism will allow women, according to its advocates, to more equitably deal with gender and race issues. With their revised feminist theory, they position themselves such that they remain ideologically acceptable by the dominant culture.

The resistance to the term "feminism" by many African American women appears not to be their misunderstanding of the definition. Rather, the resistance suggests a selective and deliberate avoidance of an association with a social movement led by a white female majority in America, grounded in a struggle against their cultural roots in the Greco-Roman male patriarchy. While it is an appropriate struggle for white women who have been denied their equality by the men of their historic ties, this is not the same struggle for African American women. The fundamental issue is whether gender-specific theory addresses the race-specific and culture-specific issues of women who might wish to work against sexism, but who are not predisposed to substituting their historic cultural identities tor a collective women's culture.

VALUES OF CONTEMPORARY WHITE FEMINISTS

What does contemporary feminism dominated by white women offer, that is similar to or different from that of the past? And does it embrace the needs and aspirations of black women? Is it moving toward an active race-gender-class focus with equity and humanism for all? And is the new black feminism compatible with contemporary or new feminism as advocated by white women? According to Mary Rogers, in her edited volume *Contemporary Feminist Theory*, "feminist theory takes shape around the dialectic between its partnered terms. "Feminist" connotes activism and shaking things up, while 'theory' connotes dispassionate scholarship and abstract ideas. Feminist theory defeats that divergence by making theory and practice collateral projects." Rogers writes that "theorists have been grouped using names like 'standpoint theorist' or 'materialist feminist' or 'womanist theorist' among other nomenclature. A women-centered approach is necessary for feminist theorizing, but it is insufficient" (Rogers 1998: 3). What are some of the commonalities for explaining what "feminist" involves?

Feminists maintain that women and men are equally entitled to all the good things a society makes available to its members—all the opportunities, rewards, respect and status, power, and responsibilities. Feminists thus believe that gender should not be a distributive mechanism in society, a basis for social hierarchy, or a means whereby some parts of people get stunted and other parts get overdeveloped. Feminism serves, then, as an "intervention in the ideology of gender" (Grant 1993: 179). Not all feminists simply seek parity with relatively privileged men. Some challenge what gender itself embodies: namely, hierarchy. Some common values driving contemporary feminists are embedded in questions about six issues:

First—Standards used to justify why some people get to the top and other people get trapped at the bottom of various hierarchies. These standards end up as preferences that get widely institutionalized (Williams 1991: 103).

Second—Hierarchical approaches to it group's problem-solving or projects. In theory and in practice, they often turn to alternative approaches such as collaborative decision-making, agreement by consensus, and cooperative modes of dividing labor and rewards. Thus, feminists often believe that hierarchy has been overdone in societies like that of the USA and seek fairer ways of getting jobs done (Rogers 1998: 4).

Third—Social justice is crucial to that of hierarchal elimination whether it is called distributive justice, equality, fairness, or equal rights. Social justice advocates that each person's dignity is being honored with their needs recognized and addressed, and they or their group's claims to extras are anchored in merits or needs widely agreed upon and open to debate among members. Closely allied to social justice is the democratic process, which requires that each person's voice be heard or at least effectively represented (ibid: 4).

Forth—Extension of responsibility beyond oneself and one's circle of loved ones, especially to those who depend heavily on the rest of us for sustenance and nurturing.

Fifth—Inclusive thinking that would embrace all women. Given the attacks on the women's movement and white feminists as racist and elitist, the reality of inclusive practices appears to be debatable.

However, some developments may have moved feminists toward inclusive stances and interactions. A part of the development of the inclusive posture has been the movement away from dualistic, binary, either/or thinking—the very thinking that pits male against female as superior against inferior, strong against weak, and rational against emotional. By and large, contemporary feminist theorists made it their business to overcome "prefeminist, either/or, polarized thinking" (Casto 1984: 169). But while feminist theorists commonly recognize that women are both old and young, monosexual and bisexual, low income and middle income, they often do not consider that "both" is problematic. Such designations suggest a pair of realities where usually there are multiple ones, such as red, yellow, brown, black, and white, or inner city, urban, suburban, rural and frontier, and the like.

Even though some contemporary feminist theorists recognize that inclusive perspectives must extend beyond dualistic usages, others have lapses. For example, in the feminist journal *Gender & Society* appeared the article "Wives and husbands: perceptions of why wives work" (Spade 1994). All the participants in the study were white. Accordingly, the article's title should have referred to *white* spouses' attitudes. This certainly would have occurred had all the participants been black.

The inclusive intentions of contemporary feminist theory attempt to embrace multiculturalism, which mandates curricular attention to the experiences, historical and contemporary, of women and men of color, lesbians and gay men of all racial and ethnic groups, and women with diverse sexual, racial, and ethnic identities. To the extent that its inclusive intentions succeed, contemporary feminist theory both feeds into and draws on multiculturalism. That connection makes for rich but problematic theorizing insofar as "many of the factors which divide women also unite some women with men" (Hartsock 1990: 158). As Joan Wallach Scott observes, feminism is "a site where differences conflict and coalesce, where common interests are articulated and contested, where identities achieve temporary stability . . . where politics and history are made" (Scott 1996: 13).

Sixth—Freedom and its close allies, liberation and self-actualization. As Mary Rogers says:

> In the long run and across diverse domains, feminists aim to enhance women's freedom to choose the circumstances and purposes of their lives. For a variety of reasons, rooted in their experiences of androcentric (male-centered) institutions, feminists mostly abhor doctrine, orthodoxy, and anything else that decontexualizes people's choice making. Disinclined to prescribe or proscribe anything specific for women, feminists commonly lean toward nonjudgmental stances about women's actual choices, even those they themselves may not favor. Feminism is not about "enlightened" women who, having raised their consciousness, then tell other women how they should live.
>
> Yet feminist theory is normative. How might these two perspectives be reconciled, at least in principle? (Rogers, 1998: 6)

Sandra Lee Bartky says feminism involves both critique and resistance (Bartky 1993: 13). Characteristically, feminists challenge whatever demeans, hurts, impedes, or otherwise treats unfairly large numbers of women. Thus, most feminist writing includes critique among its defining features. At the same time, most such writing delineates how women resist

and can further resist such unfair circumstances. All these normative concerns are macro-level. That is, they address a society's or community's social
structure, its culture (values, norms, beliefs), and diverse female groupings'
opportunities and outcomes. While normative, these concerns are large-scale
and impersonal: they have to do with systemic patterns and aggregated human activities.

In the personal and interpersonal spheres, where selfhood and relationships
are embodied, feminists turn away from normative thinking. Like many other
contemporary theorists, they recognize that each person makes choices within
a biographical situation of which one is a product that no one else can fully
apprehend; that she chooses by drawing on the resources available. Thus, one
might hear a feminist protest about the objectification of women but never
hear her criticize a real-life person who works as a fashion model. Feminists
recognize, then, that women lead "lives of multiple commitments and multiple beginnings" (Bateson 1990: 17).

Drawing on work from the sociology of knowledge, proposed by Peter L.
Berger and Thomas Luckmann's *The Social Construction of Reality* (1967),
and recent work of feminist theorists such as Dorothy E. Smith (1990), it appears that all knowledge is socially constructed and variously linked to what
Smith calls the "relations of ruling" in society. Their work suggests that theory is a product of the real world, not a creation of "pure" ideas. Zillah R.
Eisenstein extends on that notion as she posits "Theory must grow out of reality, but it must be able to pose another vision of reality as well" (Eisenstein
1979: 30). If these writers are correct, then feminists are first and foremost
shaped by the American society of which they are a part—either those privileged by their white skin or those not privileged because of lack of white skin.

AFRICAN AMERICAN WOMEN, THEIR MEN, FAMILIES, AND THE CONTEMPORARY/NEW FEMINISM

What relevance does the contemporary or new feminism hold for African
American women, based on the values being espoused by its advocates? Do
these values embrace African American women, their men, and their families? Does the new/contemporary feminism encourage action on behalf of
self and community? Does it raise difficult questions, suggest relevant alternatives, hold powerful people accountable, and empower those who desire
change? Or, is it simply a way of usurping an existing paradigm? While the
discussion on values of contemporary or new feminists—including those
new black feminists—are informative and useful, perhaps, the only true paradigms set forth for explaining and giving direction to/for black women's
lives are those set forth before the new black feminists or contemporary

white feminists—those provided by Hudson-Weems, Gordon, and other Africana womanists.

The long-standing focus on the woman and her role in the greater society continues to be at the center of controversy today. Even prior to the Civil War and the Emancipation Proclamation, women were engaged in shaping their role within the context of a particular social reality, one in which white males dominated within a racist patriarchal system. Although racism is clearly the bedrock of oppression, white women in general, and the feminist movement in particular, have both been driven almost exclusively by issues related solely to gender oppression. However, the vast majority of black women have necessarily focused their energies on combating racism first, before addressing the gender question. As a consequence, it is dear that the two groups ultimately have disparate goals for meeting their specific needs. In short, for most black women, who are family-centered, it is race empowerment; for white women, many of whom are female-centered, it is female empowerment. Because of this difference in agendas, distinct lexicons of names and definitions are critical.

Julia Hare makes a comment on the reality of the difference in the politics of black life and that of white life, particularly in terms of the difference in certain meanings and ideals relative to the two parallel groups:

> Women who are calling themselves black feminists need another word that describes what their concerns are. Black feminism is not a word that describes the plight of Black women. In fact, . . . black feminists have not even come to a true core definition of what black feminism is. The white race has a woman problem because the women were oppressed. Black people have a man and woman problem because Black men are as oppressed as their women. (quoted in Crawford 1993: 15)

In the late 1960s the Civil Rights Movement, which stressed liberation, marked the first time Africana people engaged in a struggle to resist racism where distinct boundaries were established, which separated the roles of women and men. Africana male activists publicly acknowledged expectations that women involved in the movement would conform to a subservient role pattern. This sexist expectation was expressed as women were admonished to manage household needs and breed warriors tor the revolution. Toni Cade elaborated on the issue of roles that prevailed in black organizations during the 1960s:

> It would seem that every organization you can name has had to struggle at one time or another with seemingly mutinous cadres of women getting salty about having to man the telephones or fix the coffee while the men wrote the position papers and decided on policy. Some groups condescendingly allotted two or three slots in the executive order to women. Others encouraged the sisters to form a

separate caucus and work out something that wouldn't split the organization. Others got nasty and forced the women to storm out to organize separate workshops. Over the years, things have sort of been cooled out. But I have yet to hear a coolheaded analysis of just what any particular group's stand is on the question. Invariably, I hear from some dude that Black women must be supportive and patient so that Black men can regain their manhood. The notion of womanhood, they argue—and only if pressed to address themselves to the notion do they think of it or argue—is dependent on his defining his manhood. (Cade 1970: 107–8)

Though many black women activists did not succumb to the attempts of black men to reduce them to a secondary role in the movement, many did. bell hooks writes:

Black women questioning and or rejecting a patriarchal black movement found little solace in the contemporary women's movement. For while it drew attention to the dual victimization of black women by racist and sexist oppression, white feminists tended to romanticize the black female experience rather than discuss the negative impact of oppression. When feminists acknowledge in one breath that black women are victimized and in the same breath emphasize their strength, they imply that though black women are oppressed they manage to circumvent the damaging impact of oppression by being strong—and that is simply not the case. Usually, when people talk about the "strength" of black women they are referring to the way in which they perceive black women coping with oppression. They ignore the reality that to be strong in the face of oppression is not the same as overcoming oppression, that endurance is not to be confused with transformation. (hooks 1981: 6)

Thus, to be an activist in the liberation of black people or women did not necessarily mean there was sensitivity for black women. Now, for black people to move forward as a strong group will require men and women working together to build their families, institutions, and communities (Aldridge 1991, 1992, 1998). Values espoused by contemporary or new feminist—black or white—are relevant for self-affirmation of all people. But it is not feminism that best reflects the current conditions or future needs of black women, men, children, and their communities. Rather, to build upon the paradigm of Africana womanism as a means of moving toward a more humane world may be in the best interest of black people—indeed, all people.

CONTINUING ISSUES FOR AFRICAN AMERICAN WOMEN

There is still unfinished business at the intersection of black issues and feminist issues:

- Claiming nommo or naming and self defining. Clearly, those who control the naming and defining, control the named and defined.
- Recognition that common usage of feminism or black feminism by many African American women differs within the group as well as from that of many white women, who may or may not be self-defined feminists.
- Commitment to the Black Freedom Movement over the Women's Liberation Movement because of a "best fit."
- Resolution of the tension produced by feminism and its perspective of "women's culture." This requires African women with primary identity in the African diaspora to fend off racism from both white women and white men.
- Participation in coalitions that advocate inclusion of African American women, with a gender-specific focus that obscures race-specific issues.
- Development of strategies for moving toward common grounds on crucial issues that impact women and men from different cultural groups.

Black women had no significant role in the Women's or Feminist Movement of the 1960s, even though their ideas and strategies used in the Civil Rights Movement were appropriated by white women. However, neither black women's major concerns nor historical realities were embraced. As such, a place had to be created for black women. In order to fully include them, there was need for more than writing about them. White women needed to change their attitudes and behavior toward black women, and black women were required to make their concerns known and dealt with. Black women also had to become more active in telling their own stories and moving toward changing their own conditions. It is clear that most black women organizations, writers, and/or activists were not attaching the same meanings to the concept of feminism as were most white women or their various groups.

Numerous black scholars and critics as well as lay individuals have held on to a concept that they had no part in naming or defining, rather than moving to a different one that embodies what they in actuality are now espousing— Africana womanism, or perhaps a new term of "*humanism*" (emphasis mine). The call for an intersection of race, gender, and class is important, but under the rubric of feminism it carries all the nuances of continued control by white women, who named and defined it. The new or contemporary feminism espouses values that embrace politically-correct concepts of inclusiveness, multiculturalism, and diversity. But even if the new feminism takes the uncomfortable positions of actively addressing racism, classism, and other "isms" as passionately as it has battled against sexism, will black women have the "agency" necessary to do what is best for them, their families, and communities? If so, then the quest for an authentic paradigm will have been realized, with a significant intersection of gender and race in the aftermath of the Second World War.

NOTES

From: A Companion to African American History. Alton Hornsby, Jr. (ed.) Malden, Mass. 2005, pp. 395–411. Reprinted by Permission.

BIBLIOGRAPHY

Aldridge, Delores P. (1991) Focusing: *Institutional and Interpersonal Perspectives on Black Male-Female Relations*. Chicago: Third World Press.
———. (1992) "Womanist issues in Black Studies: toward integrating of Africana women into Africana studies," *Afrocentric Scholar*. 1 (1, May).
———. (1998) "Black women and the new world order: toward a fit in the economic marketplace" in Irene Browne (ed.), *Latinas and African American Women at Work: Race, Gender, and Economic Inequality*. New York: Russell Sage Foundation, 357–79.
Aptheker, Bettina (1981) "Strong is what we make each other: unlearning racism within women's studies," *Women's Studies Quarterly* 9 (4, Winter).
Bartky, Sandra Lee (1993) "Reply to commentators on femininity and domination," *Hypatia: A Journal of Feminist Philosophy* 8 (Winter): 193.
Bateson, Mary Catherine (1990) *Composing a Life*. New York: Penguin Books.
Berger, Peter L. and Luckmann, Thomas (1967) *The Social Construction of Reality: A Treatise in the Sociology of Knowledge*. New York: Anchor Books.
Boxer, Marilyn J. (1982) "For and about women: the theory and practice of women's studies in the United States," *Signs* 7: 160–95.
Brewer, Rose (1993) "Theorizing race, class, and gender: the new scholarship of black feminist intellectuals and black women's labor" in Joy James and A. Busia (eds.), *Theorizing Black Feminisms: The Visionary Pragmatism of Black Women*, 13–30. New York: Routledge.
Brown, Elsa Barkeley (1989) "Womanist consciousness: Maggie Lena Walker and the Independent Order of Saint Luke," *Signs* 14.
Cade, Toni (ed.) (1970) *The Black Woman: An Anthology*. New York: New American Library.
Casto, Ginette ([1984] 1990) *American Feminism: A Contemporary History*, trans. Elizabeth Loverde-Bagwell. New York: New York University Press.
Collins, Patricia H. (1990) *Black Feminist Thought: Knowledge, Consciousness, and the Politics of Empowerment*, 2nd edn. London: HarperCollins Academic.
———. (1996) "What's in a name: womanism, black feminism and beyond," *Black Scholar* 26 (1, March): 9–17.

——. (1999) "Gender, black feminism and black political economy," *Annual of the American Academy of Political and Social Science*, 568: 41–53.

Combahee River Collective ([1977] 1998) "'A black feminist statement'" in Mary F. Rogers (ed.), *Contemporary Feminist Theory*, 13–15. McGraw-Hill: New York.

Crawford, Ellen (1993) ""Feminism in academe: the race factor,'" *Black Issues in Higher Education* 10 (1, March).

Crawford, Vicki L., Rouse, Jacqueline Anne, and Woods, Barbara (eds.) (1999) *Women in the Civil Rights Movement: Trailblazers and Torchbearers, 1941–1965*. Brooklyn: Carlson.

Eisenstein, Zillah R. (1979) "Introduction" in Zillah R. Eisenstein (ed.), *Capitalist Patriarchy and the Case for Socialist Feminism*. New York and London: Monthly Review Press.

Evans, Sara (1979) *Personal Politics: The Roles of Women's Liberation in the Civil Rights Movement and the New Left*. New York: Alfred A. Knopf.

Glenn, Nakano E. (1999) "The social construction and institutionalization of gender and race: an integrative framework" in M. Marx Ferree, J. Lorber, and B. B. Hess (eds.), *Revisioning Gender, 3–43*. Thousand Oaks, CA: Sage.

Gordon, Vivian V. (1991) *Black Women Feminism, and Black Liberation: Which Way?* Chicago: Third World Press.

——. (2000) "Black women, feminism, and black studies" in Delores P. Aldridge and Carlene Young (eds.), *Out of the Revolution: The Development of Africana Studies*, 165–75. Lanham, MD: Lexington.

Grant, Judith (1993) *Fundamental Feminism: Contesting the Core Concepts of Feminist Theory*. New York: Routledge.

Hartsock, Nancy (1990) "Foucault on power: a theory for women?" in Linda J. Nicholson (ed.), *Feminism/Postmodernism*. New York: Routledge.

Hemmons, Willa M. (1980) "Black women and the women's liberation movement" in LaFrances Rodgers Rose (ed.), *The Black Woman*, 285–99. Beverley Hills, CA: Sage.

hooks, bell (1981) *Ain't I A Woman: Black Women and Feminism*. Boston: South End Press.

——. (1984) *Feminist Theory: From Margin to Center*. Boston: South End Press.

——. (1989) *Talking Back: Thinking Feminist, Thinking Black*. Boston: South End Press.

Hudson-Weems, Clenora (1989) "Cultural and agenda conflicts in academia: critical issues for Africana women studies," *Western Journal of Black Studies* 13 (4): 185–9.

——. (1993) *Africana Womanism: Reclaiming Ourselves*. Detroit: Bedford.

——. (2000) "Africana womanism: an overview" in Delores P. Aldridge and Carlene Young (eds.), *Out the Revolution: The Development of Africana Studies*, 205–17. Lanham, MD: Lexington Books.

Hull, Gloria T., Scott, Patricia Bell, and Smith, Barbara (eds.) (1982) *All the Women Are White, All the Blacks are Men, but Some of Us Are Brave: Black Women's Studies*. Old Westbury, NY: Feminist Press.

James, Joy and Farmer, Ruth (eds.) (1993) *Spirit, Space, Survival: Africana American Women in (White) Academe*. New York: Routledge.

James, S. and Busia, A. (1993) *Theorizing Black Feminisms: The Visionary Pragmatism of Black Women*. New York: Routledge.

Loewenberg:, Bert J. and Bogin, Ruth (eds.) (1976) *Black Women in Nineteenth-Century American Life*. University Park: Pennsylvania State Press.

Lorber, Judith (1994) *Paradoxes of Gender*. New Haven, CT: Yale University Press.

——. (1998) *Gender Inequality: Feminist Theories and Politics*. Los Angeles: Roxbury.

Mohanty, Carolyn (1991) "Under western eyes: feminist scholarship and colonial discourses" in C. Mohanty, A. Russo, and L. Torres (eds.), *Third World Women and the Politics of Feminism*. Bloomington: Indiana University Press.

Morrison, Toni (1987) *Beloved*. New York: Alfred A. Knopf.

Owens, Timothy J., Mortimer, Heylan T., and Finch, Michael D. (1996) "Self-determination as a source of self-esteem in adolescence," *Social Forces* 74 (4, June).

Rogers, Mary F. (1998) Contemporary Feminist Theory. New York: McGraw-Hill.

Rouse, Jacqueline A. (1989) *Lagenia Burns Hope: Black Southern Reformer*. Athens: University of Georgia Press.

Scott, Joan Wallach (1996) "Introduction" in Joan Wallach Scott (ed.), *Feminism and History*. New York: Oxford University Press.

Shaw, Stephanie J. (1996) *What a Woman Ought to Be and to Do: Black Professional Women during the Jim Crow Era*. Chicago: University of Chicago Press.

Smith, Barbara (1982) "Racism and women's studies" in G. T. Hull, P. B. Scott, and B. Smith (eds.), *All the Women Are White, All the Blacks Are Men, But Some of Us Are Brave: Black Women's Studies*. New York: Feminist Press.

Smith, Dorothy E. (1990) *The Conceptual Practices of Power: A Feminist Sociology of Knowledge*. Boston: Northeastern University Press.

Spade, Joan V. (1994) "Wives and husbands: perceptions of why wives work," *Gender and Society* 8 (2, June): 170–88.

Spelman, E. (1988) *Inessential Woman: Problems of Exclusion in Feminist Thought*. Boston: Beacon Press.

Stefano, Christine Di (1991) "Who the heck are we? Theoretical turns against gender," *Frontiers* 12 (2): 87.

Walker, Alice (1982) *The Color Purple*. New York: Washington Square Press.

——. (1983) *In Search of Our Mothers' Gardens: Womanist Prose*. New York: Harcourt Brace, Jovanovich.

Williams, Patricia J. (1991) *The Alchemy of Race and Rights*. Cambridge, MA: Harvard University Press.

Zinn, Baca M. and Dill, Thornton B. (1996) "Theorizing difference from multiracial feminism," *Feminist Studies* 22: 321–33.

SUGGESTIONS FOR FURTHER READING

Baumgardner, Jennifer and Richards, Amy (2000) *Manifesta: Young Women, Feminism, and the Future*. New York: Farrar, Straus, & Giroux.

Bell, Brandi Leigh-Ann (2002) "Riding the third wave: women-produced zines and feminisms," *Resources for Feminist Research*, 29: 3–4.

Dicker, Rory and Piepmeier, Alison (eds.) (2003) *Catching a Wave: Reclaiming Feminism for the 21st Century*. Boston: Northeastern University Press.

Drake, Jennifer (1997) "Third wave feminisms," *Feminist Studies*, 23: 1.

Findlen, Barbara (ed.) (1995) *Listen Up! Voices from the Next Feminist Generation*. Seattle: Seal.

Franklin, V. P. (2002) "Hidden in plain view: African American women, radical feminism, and the origins of women studies programs, 1967–1974," *Journal of African American History*, 87 (Fall): 433–45.

Gordon, Vivian V. (1991) *Black Women, Feminism, and Black Liberation: Which Way?* Chicago: Third World Press.

Green, Karen and Taormino, Tristan (eds.) (1997) *A Girl's Guide to Taking Over the World: Writings from the Girl Zine Revolution*. New York: St. Martin's Press.

Heywood, Leslie and Drake, Jennifer (eds.) (1994) Teaching to Transgress: Education as the Practice of Freedom. New York: Routledge.

——. (1997) Third Wave Agenda: Being Feminist, Doing Feminism. Minneapolis: University of Minnesota Press.

Hudson-Weems, Clenora (1993) *Africana Womanism: Reclaiming Ourselves*. Detroit: Bedford.

Lotz, Amanda D. (2003) "Communicating third-wave feminism and new social movements: challenges for the next century of feminist endeavor," *Women and Language* 26 (1).

Manzano, Angie (2000) "Charlie's Angels: free-market feminism," *off our backs*, 30 (11).

Walker, Rebecca (ed.) (1995) *To Be Real: Telling the Truth and Changing the Face of Feminism*. New York: Anchor Books.

Appendix F

Black Women, Feminism, and Black Studies

Vivian Verdell Gordon

THE CONCEPTUAL FRAME OF REFERENCE

A people's definition of self and role is the most fundamental statement of their social reality. For African Americans today, as it has been in the past, the social reality continues to be a highly diversified daily confrontation with race based upon positions of white dominance and black subordination. The prevailing attitudes and behaviors experienced by African Americans are those that presume a relegated place of subordination through the institutionalized patterns of American stratification well rooted in racism. It is a pattern of sanctioned structured inequality.

Although the form of the devastation of racism has differed from time to time and from region to region, the net result has been and continues to be a relentless systematic imposition of unfair advantages based upon skin privilege. Reflected by its highly sophisticated patterns of pigmentocracy variously accepted and sanctioned, racism in America has been especially experienced by all persons of the African diaspora: from the newborn to the child; from the youth to the elderly; from the well-educated elite to the undereducated; from the strong to the weak; from the richer to the poorer, the dispossessed, and the homeless; from the celebrated to the unknown; from the white skinned (if they dared to identify with race and culture) to the ebony hued; from the striving assimilationist to the most avid separatist.

Of primary importance to the focus of this discussion is the fact that racism has not been gender-specific in America. The power group's psychocultural conceptual references of "black as bad" and "white as good" have been visited with equal rage upon both African-American men and women. The legend of history as well as contemporary research clearly establishes that in the matter of color, women out of the African diaspora have been black first and female second.

Thus, African-American women have been victimized by those same indignities and inequities of racism as have been African-American men. In fact, given the particular record of the sexual exploitation of African American women at the hands of the owners during the time of the enslavement, and their continued disproportionate physical and economic abuse, it can be established that Africana women have been thrice victimized: by racism, sexism, and economic exploitation. Racism, sexism, and economic oppression are so pervasively entwined in America, black women often have difficulty identifying which negative factor of their "self" is the primary cause of their oppression at any given time. Indeed, most often, these three oppressive forces impact upon Africana women simultaneously and equally relentlessly.

Moreover, these black females, my historic women of kin, have been selectively female only under those conditions that allowed them to provide profits for persons of power, whether that profit be the imposed products of their reproduction, which benefited their slave owners, or whether it be the more modern benefits of their relative positions of structured "feminized poverty" in the market of today. An analysis of the American power dynamics unquestionably establishes this inequality among Africana women.[1]

Obviously, if Africana women were to elect to do so, they could lay an unprecedented historic claim to the lexicon "feminist" by simply citing the conditions over which they have struggled in the Americas, such as: (1) the right to control one's own reproduction; (2) freedom from sexual harassment; (3) equality before the law; (4) the right to vote; (5) equal pay for equal work (or historically, pay for work); (6) equal opportunity for a quality education; (7) quality housing; (8) quality health care, including preventive and rehabilitation services; (9) survivors' benefits for families; (10) old age security; (11) nonpunitive assistance programs for the qualified poor; and (12) the abolition of racism and sexism in the criminal justice system.

Clearly, their rebellion during the enslavement; their devotion to family; their copartnership with men in the fight against oppression; their demonstrated ability to do work, including "traditional man's work"; their historic organization, which demonstrates an ability to organize on behalf of the elevation of positions of women; their involvement in the development of educational and business institutions, as well as their contributions to science, medicine, and technology from the times of the ancients to the present; more than qualify Africana women as the first "feminists." That they have continuously elected to not compartmentalize their identity into categories of race versus gender specificity, therefore, becomes the next important issue for discussion. It is a discussion and identity that must begin with the "word."

NOMMO: THE WORD FOR BLACK WOMEN

A fundamental place to begin the destruction of a people's culture is with the denial of their symbols. It is the meanings associated with symbols that are vital not only to cultural understanding and communication, but also to the ultimate cultural continuity. Nommo, or "the word," represents a people's manipulation of their symbols for the definitions of self and role, as well as their rooted place in the divine order of things. Thus, the resilience and resourcefulness of Africana people can best be understood through a lens that telescopes to the African cultural conceptual underpinnings of the maat-ian (Egyptian) thought. It is the maat, which has endured from the time of the ancients to the present, that provides both black men and women with a point of departure, for actualization as males and females.

It is not simply sloganistic for African Americans to state as their definition, "Because We Are, Therefore I Am." Moreover, that very key concept—the maat—directs us to collective consciousness that demands the abandonment of the internalized sexism of lexicon of power that defends male supremacy and female subordination. Therefore, any discussion about Black Studies and feminism must begin with a clear discussion about the symbolic meanings and differences between the lexicon of feminism and the word nommo.

The lexicon of feminism is conceptually exclusive. It is seated in a gender-specific identity, which is a female response to the unique experiences of a male supremacy that America is justified by a culturally rooted belief system that traces back to a Greco-Roman legacy. The Word, or nommo, seated in the maat, as previously discussed, requires the co-principles of the male and female as the proper placement of meaning for the people. The proper use of the Word or nommo, like the correct process of naming, is the means by which African Americans link to their ancestral past and at the same time initiate directional guides for the future. Thus for African-American women, sociopolitical transformation has always been highlighted by their identification with the total community—which is ultimately the extended kin, as opposed to an ongoing isolated gender-specific identity.

One need only to briefly review that which African-American women have both endured, survived, and progressed while simultaneously transforming themselves, their kinships, and their communities. Consider for example the politics of language and naming evidenced by the signs on segregated doors that read "White Ladies" and "Colored Women" during the times of apartheid of the American South. Emancipating themselves and liberating their thinking from that of the colonialist, African-American women have laid claim (although often subconsciously) to the maat in their individual and organizational struggles. The various use of names such as "Colored Ladies" or "Negro Women" in early organizations is evidence of this transformational naming process.

Thus, to begin any discussion of feminism and Black Studies, without immediately taking into consideration the importance of nommo in the African and the African-American tradition, is to attempt to discuss the question of African-American women and feminism, or Black Studies and feminism, without giving separate attention to the politics of language in the process of identity. Clearly, overt resistance to the term feminism by so many African-American women is not their misunderstanding of the definition of the term in common usage. Rather, it is an important statement of identity and politics. It is a selective and deliberate avoidance by African-American women of an association with a social movement for that female majority in America that has been in struggle against their cultural roots in the Greco-Roman male patriarchy. It is a rightful struggle of such majority women who have been denied their equality and the sexist inhumanity by the men of their historic ties. Even as those out of the African culture in America have fought against the overt ravages of racism, such as presented in the beginning of this discussion, African-American women have fought along with black men against the identification with the oppressor, which has resulted in the internalization among the people of the power dynamics of that Greco-Roman patriarchy. This definition of self—the nommo—as a point of cultural reference has been a special point of consciousness for black women in Black Studies.

BLACK WOMEN AND BLACK STUDIES

The earliest Black Studies programs on white university campuses resulted from the protest movements of the late 1950s and 1960s. In many instances, Black Studies began as a means of quieting the demands of black students who objected to the traditional academic isolation of their study from the world that was their social reality. While sharing some of the concerns of protesting white students of that same time, such as the issues of war and peace, the environment, freedom of speech, and others, black students also pointed to the unaddressed issues of racism and socio economic inequality both in their courses of study and in their educational environments. Out of these tumultuous times, academically sound programs of study and service through programs and departments of Black Studies emerged.[2]

Black women students and black women faculty, along with black women community activists joined with their male peers—their brothers in the struggle—in those protests and other efforts that contributed to the establishment of what is now emerging as the discipline of Africana Studies. Those women, like their male copartners, understood the amazon tasks before them across the nation, in the accomplishment of meaningful Black Studies with strong academic foundations within higher education.

It is also a matter of record that in many instances those new programs became male centered in their curriculum focus, which is again evidence of the extent to which African Americans, even in higher education, have internalized the traditional concept of "the academy" as a place for the study of history, even as Black Studies attempted to depart from the entrenched Eurocentric curriculum focus. The complete infusion of women as equal partners in the African-American experience remains to be accomplished, although in increasing numbers Black Studies curricula have been expanded to include some course (most often a single specialized course) about black women. In this sense, just as the infusion of the contributions of continental Africa and African Americans remains to become a part of the educational curriculum in our schools, the infusion of study by and about black women into Black Studies is vital.

Although many black women have been victimized by an unanticipated sexism by black men, including many who loudly condemn the European stranglehold upon education, such women in Black Studies have often found extensive support from others of their male and female peers who have worked together to combat such destructive forces. Overwhelmingly, against many odds, black women in Black Studies have maintained their commitment to the dynamics of the emergence of Africana Studies.

It should be remembered that black women have been actively involved both in the initiation of, as well as in the continuity and development of, Black Studies. Frequently, such women were the founders of Black Studies on their college and university campuses where, like men, they have served variously as program directors or as department chairpersons.

Black women are prominent among the persons who have served in leadership roles in the professionalization of the discipline. They are among those persons who have served for more than one term in the top position of leadership of the National Council of Black Studies, as evidenced by the esteem within that organization for Dr. Bertha Maxwell Roddy and Dr. Delores P. Aldridge.

It is also important to note that black women scholars have been extensively involved in serious Black Studies scholarship, much of which has not been simply gender-specific. As teachers and research scholars, black women have been among those on the cutting edge in the development of models and paradigms for Black Studies, as well as in the reevaluation of the applicability of selective research methodologies.[3]

Moreover, contrary to a prevailing myth, black women in Black Studies have not been limited to, nor have they sought to limit themselves to, only courses about the history of black women or the development of courses that focus upon a highly selected group of "black feminist" writers.

Also, in numerous instances, black women along with their male peers have often found themselves at odds, professionally and personally, with some black women faculty in Black Studies and in Women's Studies who have internalized an anti-male view as the gender-based response to sexism. Again, it should be understood that black women in Black Studies do not presume that the perspectives of white feminist theory are wrong or not worthy of validation through research and study. Black women simply wish to clarify that such feminist theory is an inappropriate model for Africana women who have never shared the same nature of experiences with sexism as the women of the dominant group.

The validation of the credibility of the need for inclusion or issues of Africana women into Black Studies curricula does not rest upon a denigration of Eurocentric Women's Studies. Rather, black women in Black Studies call upon all of those involved to clear become African centered and to remember the egalitarianism of the ancient African civilizations. Thus, the range of black women's experiences from the time of those ancient civilizations to the current issues of racism, sexism, and economic exploitation as particularly experienced by black women must be researched and evaluated with respect to plans for policy and action.

Extensively, black male scholars who have dominated in Black Studies, and in particular, many of those who have been the most vocal about Afrocentricity and/or African-centeredness in their presentations to the black community, have within their departments and their networks excluded appropriate attention to the paradigms that allow for study about the culturally defined sex roles that have origins in the concepts of the maat and originate in ancient African civilizations. Such exclusion must not only end as practiced by selected black male leaders in Black Studies as they function within higher education, but also as such males function as national African-female personship.

The egalitarian nature of the male/female relationship in ancient African civilizations was pervasive in families. Such research also has particular meaning for directions in studies concerned with the contemporary African-American family and male/female relationships. As the Egyptologist Barbara Lesko reports:

> Egyptian women were certainly not hesitant to appear in public, whether as merchants in the public market place or on the picket line supporting their husbands in the first recorded labor strike in history.

Indeed when we take the trouble to examine Egyptian records, our understanding of the social condition of the ancient Egyptian woman is a far cry from the "human misery" imagined by the classicist Edith Hamilton. The woman of ancient Greece was indeed in a pitiable plight, cloistered at home with her distaff while the men of her society filled the markets, theaters, stadia, and lawcourts. Nor were Greek husbands and wives found together, sharing life's trials and delights as respected and equal citizens in their secular and religious communities, enjoying equality under the law as well. SURELY THIS WAS ONE OF THE GLORIES OF ANCIENT EGYPT.[4]

The elder scholar of ancient African civilizations, John Henrik Clarke, writes:

Before going directly to the subject, "African Warrior Queens," I feel that there is a need to call attention to the historical status of African women and their contribution to the development of African societies, in order for them to be better understood as Warrior Queens in defense of their respective nations.

[The African woman's place] was not only with her family; she often ruled nations with unquestionable authority. Many African women were great militarists and on occasion led their armies in battle. Long before they knew of the existence of Europe the Africans had produced a way of life where men were secure enough to let women advance as far as their talent would take them.[5]

Writing about "Hypatia and Women's Rights in Ancient Egypt," Beatrice Lumpkin reports:

We can make one more important, historical deduction. The highly public nature of Hypatia's career was consistent with the African tradition of Egyptian women. A tradition of equal rights and very different from the oppressed position of women in classical Greek society.

Although Egyptians in Alexandria received discriminatory treatment from their Roman rulers, they were allowed to continue most of their Egyptian traditions. . . . Egyptian women thus retained most of their former rights. Indeed the African tradition of equality for women remained strong in all periods of ancient Egypt and among all social classes. In this respect, the status of women compared favorably with the status of women in some modern societies.

Nor was Hypatia the only prominent Egyptian woman scientist. Almost 1,000 years earlier, Sais, a fine medical school included many women students and faculty, especially in their section on gynecology and obstetrics.[6]

It should also be noted that there is extensive documentation to support the equal and legal and property rights of ancient African women in Egypt. It suffices to say that the evidence abounds to support the paradigm of Africana women's legacy of equal status with men. In a well-researched discussion that gives emphasis to the reports by Clarke, Lesko, and others, the researcher Clegg reports:

> Even by today's Western standards Egyptian women were free and independent and enjoyed status nearly equal to that of men. Their significance to the very fabric of society is borne out by the fact that the familiar line of descent was passed on by females. The same standard of dress applied to men and women. Hence, women were sometimes depicted stripped to the waist or wearing comfortable transparent clothes suitable to their occupations or the occasion.[7]

Of particular importance to this discussion is the research about the legal status of ancient Egyptian women. Lesko reports:

> Four thousand years ago women in the Nile Valley enjoyed more legal rights and privileges than women have in some nations of the world today. Equal pay for equal work is a cry heard now but seems to have been the norm thousands of years ago in Egypt. Whether as a full-time worker, or as a head of household and manager of a family's affairs, or as an active participant among the clergy in the religious hierarchies, the ancient Egyptian woman held a vital place in her society that amazed foreign contemporaries who observed her.
>
> The State called upon both men and women to do compulsory service as their due as citizens. The participation of a free Egyptian woman (daughter of a scribe and thus not of the peasant class) in the State corvee is documented by a Middle Kingdom papyrus and more than anything else demonstrates the official view that women and men were of equal worth, were equally obligated as subjects, and were equally capable of rendering useful service to the nation. Officially, the view was that "women's place" was not only in the home.
>
> Women were equally obligated with men as citizens of the state, and equal legal rights operated in the private sphere as well.
>
> The ancient Egyptian woman was able to testify in court, even representing herself and her siblings (both male and female) in a legal capacity before a judge. She could be appointed by the court as an executrix for an estate as well. She witnessed documents, executed her own last testament, herited, bought administered and sold property, bought and freed slaves, adopted children and sued (even her own father in one case from c. 1780 B.C.). What is more, she was able to act alone and never required a male co-signatory.[8]

Therefore, the perspective from which discussions about Black Studies and Africana women occurs is that which acknowledges this ancient African legend of egalitarianism. For black women this is the correct point of departure—that of culture and role. It is the conceptual source of our name.

BLACK WOMEN AND WOMEN'S STUDIES

It is a matter of record that the black student protests resulted in the formalized programs of Black Studies on predominantly white college and university campuses. Similarly, those programs have provided the model for many other culture-specific programs as well as the gender-specific program that has become formalized as Women's Studies.

Primarily initiated in the 1960s, the formalized programs of Women's Studies resulted from yet another challenge to the traditional male-centered university curriculum. Maintaining that there is a women's culture, many would also say that Women's Studies is both a gender-specific and culture-specific program. Presenting themselves in a "woman as nigger" paradigm, Women's Studies advocates have pressured successfully in higher education to advance the academic validity of a feminist theory, albeit one that it speaks to their second-class historic status and their contemporary social subordination.

Appropriately, many black women have extreme difficulty with Women's Studies and the perspective of "women's culture," for their primary identity remains that of the African diaspora. Repeatedly, they reflect upon the value they have historically placed upon their struggle to maintain cultural traditions, often enduring the overt racism of white women who have shared and benefited from their skin-privilege links, and their cultural ties to the white male power club. Programs in Women's Studies have not addressed the Eurocentric nature of higher education's cultural imperialism, although the newer feminist theory does address European women's roles in the emergence of Western world culture.

Although some Women's Studies programs have advocated curricula of inclusion to include some attention to the history of women of color or so-called third world women, the most fundamental issue is whether or not it is appropriate for Women's Studies gender-specific theory to be presumed to address the race-specific and culture-specific issues of women who might wish to work against sexism, but who certainly do not wish to substitute their historic cultural identifies for a so-called collective women's culture.

This is certainly a key issue for black women for whom white women have been an aggressive part of oppression. More importantly, it is counterproductive to the struggle for black liberation from racism as it impacts upon all people out of the African diaspora. In view of the structure of the academy, and in view of the nature of sexism in America, it is appropriate that some issue-specific, time-limited coalitions be formed between black women, white women and other women of color; however, the surrender of the study of women, including the formation of theories that ignore the cultural diversity of women and their wish to maintain such identity is highly inappropriate.

In some instances the initiation of Women's Studies presents a direct threat to the already established but often inadequately funded and academically buffeted Black Studies. Frequently using budget issues (even in times when there have not been crisis), traditional university structures maintain the "new" Women's Studies programs have to share in their already scarce dollars for "minority studies." Thus, from the perspectives of the liberation struggle, cultural relevance, and competition for the higher education dollar, we can observe how in the majority of situations the emergence of Women's Studies is viewed with serious concern by black women committed to Black Studies. There is clear evidence that throughout higher education, the more recently established Women's Studies programs have excelled—even in tight budget times—while such budget limitations have provided prime arguments for the continued limitations placed upon Black Studies.[9]

This situation is further compounded by American racism, which results in declining financial resources for Black Studies, and thus an increasingly declining number of professional university graduates needed for Black Studies, as well as faculty, throughout the academy. The same reports, which indicate increased financial support for Women's Studies and diminished support for Black Studies, indicates the continued devastation impact upon black student graduate study resulting from increased tuition and student fees, and diminished race-specific financial support through special grants and loans. The Bush administration's attack, in the 1980s, upon special financial assistance for "minority and Black students" could have consequences for the future.

Although there is little debate about the sexism that has limited all women in higher education and in America, black women in Black Studies are aware of the more extensive resource pool from which white women faculty emerge, compared to that for all black scholars-male and female-and the extent to which black women have been scapegoated as the primary benefactors of affirmative action.[10] As supported by the study *A Common Destiny*, within higher education as within the general marketplace, white women have been the primary benefactors of the push for "minority" inclusion and have displaced not only white males, but also black males, and black females.

NOTES

From *Out of the Revolution: The Development of Africana Studies*. Delores P. Aldridge and Carlene Young (eds.). Lexington Books: Lanham, Maryland, 2000, pp. 165–175. Reprinted by Permission.

1. Vivian V. Gordon, *Black Women, Feminism, Block Liberation: Which Way?* (Chicago: Third World Press, 1991).

2. Vivian V. Gordon, "The Coming of Age of Black Studies," *Western Journal of Black Studies* 5, no. 3 (fall 1981). See also *Black Studies in the 80s: Beyond Relevance* (New York: Jossey-Bass Press, 1981).

3. Vivian V. Gordon, "Theoretical and Methodological Perspectives for the Longitudinal Study of Black Communities" (proceedings of Southern Sociological Society, April 1979). For other articles relevant to the issues of research and methodology, see the various indices references for the *Western Journal of Black Studies*, the *Journal of Black Studies*, the *Journal of Black Psychology*, *Phi Delta Kappan*, and other appropriate journals. See also *Black Studies: Theory, Method, and Cultural Perspectives*, ed. Talmadge Anderson (Pullman, Wash.: Washington State University Press, 1990).

4. Barbara S. Lesko, *The Remarkable Women of Ancient Egypt* (Providence, R.I.: B.C. Scribe Publications, 1987).

5. John H. Clarke, "African Warrior Queens," in *Black Women in Antiquity,* ed. Ivan Van Sertima (New Brunswick, N.J.: Transaction Books, 1986).

6. Beatrice Lumpkin, "Hypatia and Women's Rights in Ancient Egypt," in *Black Women in Antiquity*, ed. Ivan Van Sertima (New Brunswick, N.J.: Transaction Books, 1986). For additional information about women in ancient African civilizations, see selected appropriate references listed in *Kemet and Other Ancient African Civilizations*, comp. Vivian V. Gordon, with a foreword by Asa G. Hilliard III.

7. Legrand H. Clegg and Karima Y. Ahmed, "Egypt during the Golden Age," in *When Black Men Ruled the World*, ed. Ivan Van Sertima (New Brunswick, N.J., Transaction Books, 1987).

8. Lesko, *The Remarkable Women of Ancient Egypt*.

9. Whereas individual department budgets have been variously impacted by the present economic crisis, it can be documented that during the same period of time, programs and departments of Women's Studies have continued to advance. Although not a discussion presented on this issue, a detail of the patterns of growth of diverse programs in higher education presents the comparative data to which reference is made here. See the Chronicle of Higher Education, May 1992. Additionally, data to support the economic inequality between black and white women in higher education and other employment as well as the gains by white women resulting from affirmative action programs of the past ten years may be found in Committee on the Status of Black Americans, Commission on Behavioral and Social Sciences and Education, National Research Council, *A Common Destiny: Blacks and American Society* (Washington, D. C.: The National Academy Press, 1989).

10. Committee on the Status of Black Americans, *A Common Destiny*.

Bibliography

Aldridge, Delores P. "On Race and Culture: Beyond Afrocentrism and Eurocentrism to Cultural Democracy." *Sociological Focus* 33, no.

Aldridge, Delores P. "Black Women and the New World Order: Toward a Fit in the Economic Marketplace," Pp. 357–379 in *Latinas and African American Women at Work: Race, Gender, and Economic Inequality,* edited by Irene Browne. New York: Russell Sage Foundation, 1999.

———. "Grace Towns Hamilton, 1907–1992." in *Black Women in America: An Historical Encyclopedia,* edited by Darlene Clark Hines et al. Brooklyn, New York: Carlson Publishing, 1993.

———. *Focusing: Black Male-Female Relationships*. Chicago: Third World Press, 1991.

Aldridge, Delores P., ed. *Black Male-Female Relationships: A Resource Book of Selected Materials*. Dubuque, Iowa: Kendall/Hunt Publishing Company, 1989.

Aldridge, Delores P. "Toward a New Role and Function of Black Studies in White and Historically Black Institutions," *Journal of Negro Education* (Summer 1984): 359–367.

———. "Litigation and Education of Blacks: Another Look at the U.S. Supreme Court," *The Journal of Negro Education*, vol. xlvii, no.1, (Winter 1978).

Aldridge, Delores P. "Teaching About Black American Families," *Journal Of Social Education*, 41, no. 6, (October 1977).

Aldridge, Delores P. and Carlene Young (eds). *Out of the Revolution: The Development of Africana Studies*. Lanham, MD: Lexington Books, 2000.

Aldridge, Delores P. and Rodgers-Rose, LaFrancis, eds. *River of Tears: The Politics of Black Women's Health*. Newark, NJ: Traces Publishing, 2003.

Aldridge, Delores P. and Dowell, Peter. "Bridging the Gap: The Challenge of Interfacing American and Afro-American Studies." Pp. in *Character and Culture in a Changing World*, edited by John Hague. Westport, Connecticut: Greenwood Press, 979.

Asante, Molefi K. *The Afrocentric Idea*. Philadelphia, PA.: Temple University Press, 1987.

Azibo, Daudi Ajani ya. "Articulating the Distinction between Black Studies and the Study of Blacks: The Fundamental Role of Culture and the African-Centered Worldview." Pp. 420–441 in *The African American Studies Reader* edited by Nathaniel Norment, Jr. Durham North Carolina: Carolina Academic Press, 2001.

Blackwell, James E. *The Black Community: Diversity and Unity*. New York: Harper & Row, 1985.

——. "Minorities in the Liberation of ASA?" *The American Sociologist*. 23 (Spring 1992): 11–17.

Blackwell, James E. *Mainstreaming Outsiders: The Production of Black Professionals*. Bayside, New York: General Hall, Inc., 1981.

Blackwell, James E. and Morris Janowitz, eds. *Black Sociologists: Historical and Contemporary Perspectives*. Chicago: The University of Chicago Press, 1974.

Brewer, Rose M. "Black Women and Feminist Sociology: The Emerging Perspective." *The American Sociologist*, (Spring 1989): 57–70.

Carby, Hazel V. *Reconstructing Womanhood: The Emergence of the Afro-American Woman Novelist*. New York: Oxford University Press, 1987.

Communi-K November 11, 1996. 29(6)"Sociology professor develops racial harassment policy." Lexington, Kentucky.

Community Voice Newsjournal. "UK Sociology professor develops racial harassment policy" 9(13) Oct. 18–Nov.1, 1996.

Conyers, James E. "Black American Doctorates in Sociology: A follow-up Study of Their Social and Educational Origins," In *The Sociology of African Americans: A Reader* edited by Clyde O. McDaniel, Jr. Fort Worth: Harcourt Brace, 1994.

——. "The Association of Black Sociologists: A Descriptive Account from an "Insider." *The American Sociologist* 23 (Spring): 49–55.

Collins, Patricia Hill. *Black Feminist Thought: Knowledge, Consciousness, and the Political Empowerment*. New York: Routledge, 1990.

Cooper, Anna J. *A Voice From the South: By A Black Woman of the South*. Xenia, Ohio: Aldine, 1892.

Deegan, M. J., ed. *Women in Sociology: A Bio-Bibliographical Sourcebook*. New York: Greenwood, 1991.

Dennis, Rutledge. 1988. "The Use of Participant-Observation in Race Relations Research." *Race and Ethnic Relations*, 5: 25–46.

Diggs, Mary H. "Some Problems and Needs of Negro Children as Revealed by Comparative Delinquency and Crime Statistics." *Journal of Negro Education*, no.19, 290–97.

Dooley, Karla. "Conference Salutes UK's Original Trailblazers," *Kentucky Kernel*. March 30, 1999.

Du Bois, W. E. B. 1903. *The Souls of Black Folk*. Greenwich, Conn.: Fawcett Publications, Inc.

Du Bois, W. E. B. *The Autobiography of W. E. B. Du Bois*. New York: Torch Publications, 1968.

Edelman, Marian Wright. *The Measure of Our Success: A Letter to My Children and Yours.* Boston: Beacon Press, 1992.

Epstein, Cynthia Fuchs. "Positive Effects of the Multiple Negative: Explaining the Success of Black Professional women." *American Journal of Sociology* 78 no. 4 (1973): 912–935.

Etzkowitz, Henry. 1988. "The Contradictions of Radical Sociology." *Critical Sociology*, 15, no. 2, (Summer): 95–113.

Ferris, Susan. December 12, 1993. "Mounting Campaign to keep immigrants out: Group's stated aim to cap population walks fine line of bigotry, critics say." The *San Francisco Examiner.* The Hearst Corporation: A-1.

Froelich, Suzanne *UK News.* Feb 16, 1994. "Exhibit Celebrates African American Women.

Frye, Marilyn. 1992. "Oppression," *Race, Class, and gender: An Anthology.* Edited by Margaret L. Andersen and Patricia Hill Collins. Belmont, California: Wadsworth Publishing Company.

Gaines, K. K. 1996. *Uplifting the Race: Black Leadership. Politics, and Culture in the Twentieth Century.* Princeton, NJ: Princeton University Press.

Gordon, Vivian Verdell. 1991. Unpublished Vitae.

———. 1990. "Black Women, Feminism and Black Studies." Unpublished Paper.

———. 1985. *Black Women, Feminism and Black Liberation: Which Way?* Chicago: Third World Press.

———. 1981. "The Coming of Age of Black Studies." *The Western Journal of Black Studies* 5 (3): 231–236.

———. 1980. *The Self-Concept of Black Americans.* New York: University Press of America.

———. 1979. *Lectures: Black Scholars on Black Issues.* New York: University Press of America.

———. 1995. SUNY-Albany Obituary Desk. Unpublished Obituary Note.

Giddings, Paula. 1984. *When and Where I Enter: The Impact of Black Women on Race and Sex in America.* New York: Morrow.

Hamilton, Ruth S. "The Savannah Story: Education and Desegregation." In *Our Children's Children*, edited by Raymond W. Mack, pp. 109–40. New York: Random House, 1968.

Hamilton, Ruth S. *Urbanization in West Africa.* Evanston, Illinois: Northwestern University Press, 1965.

Hill, Adelaide C. "Negro Fertility and Family Size Preferences: Implications for Programming of Health and Social Services." In *The Negro American*, edited by Talcott Parsons and Kenneth B. Clark, pp. 205–24, Cambridge, Massachusetts: Houghton Mifflin, 1966.

Higginbotham, Elizabeth. 1993. "Employment for Professional Black Women in the Twentieth Century." in *Ingredients for Women's Employment Policy.* Christine Bose and Glenna Spitze (eds). Albany: State University of New York Press.

Hooks, Bell. 1989. "Black and Female: Reflections on Graduate School." in *Talking Back: Thinking Feminist, Thinking Black.* Boston: South End Press.

Hooks, Bell. 1981. *Ain't I a Woman: Black Women and Feminism.* Boston: South End Press.

Hooks, Bell. 1995. *Killing Rage: Ending Racism.* New York: Henry Holt and Company.

Hooks, Bell. 1998. "White Oppression is to Blame for Black Inequality," *Inequality.* San Diego, California: Greenhaven Press, Inc., pp. 166–174.

Hudson-Weems, Clenora. 1993. *Africana Womanism: Reclaiming Ourselves.* Troy, Michigan: Bedford Publishers, Inc.

Hughes, H. M. (1975). Women in Academic Sociology, 1925–75. *Sociological Focus*, 8, no. 3: 215–222.

Hyer, Marjorie. October 24, 1980. "Experts Fear Explosion Between Hispanics and Blacks." *The Washington Post*: B8.

Jackson, Jacquelyne. 1971. 'But Where are the Men?" *The Black Scholar*, 2: 30–41.

Jackson, Jacquelyne. 1974. "Black Female Sociologists," *Black Sociologists: Historical and Contemporary Perspectives*, Blackwell, James and Janowitz, Morris, eds.: 267–295. Chicago, Ill.: University of Chicago Press.

Jackson, Jacquelyne J. "Aged Blacks: A Potpourri Towards the Reduction of Racial Inequities." *Phylon* 32 (1971): 260–80.

Jackson, Jacquelyne J. "Aged Negroes: Their Cultural Departures from Statistical Stereotypes and Selected Rural-Urban Differences." *The Gerontologist* 10 (1970): 140–45. Reprinted in *Research Planning and Action for the Elderly*, edited by Donald P. Kent, Robert Kastenbaum, and Sylvia Sherwood, pp. 501–13.

Jackson, Jacquelyne J. "The Association of Social and Behavioral Scientists." *Race* 13 (1971–72): 93–94.

Jackson, Jacquelyne J. "The Blacklands of Gerontology." *Aging and Human Development 2* (1971): 156–71.

Jackson, Jacquelyne J. "Black Professional Organizations: A Case Study." *The Journal of Afro American I Issues* 1 (1972): 75–91.

Jackson, Jacquelyne J. "Black Women in a Racist Society." In *Racism and Mental Health*, edited by Charles V. Willie, Bernard Kramer, and Bertram Brown. Pittsburgh: University of Pittsburgh Press, 1973.

Jackson, Jacquelyne J. "But Where Are the Men?" *The Black Scholar* 3 (1971): 30–41.

Jackson, Jacquelyne J. "Comparative Lifestyles and Family and Friend Relationships Among Older Black Women." *The Family Coordinator* 21 (1972): 477–85.

Jackson, Jacquelyne J. "Compensatory Care for the Black Aged." *Occasional Papers in Gerontology.* No.10. Institute of Gerontology, The University of Michigan-Wayne State University, pp. 15–23.

Jackson, Jacquelyne J. "Family Organization and Ideology." in *Comparative Studies of Blacks and Whites in the United States, 1966–1970*, edited by Ralph M. Dreger and Kent S. Miller. New York: Academic Press, 1972.

Jackson, Jacquelyne J. "Kinship Relations Among Negro Americans." *Journal of Social and Behavior Sciences* 16 (1970): 5–17.

Jackson, Jacquelyne J. "Marital Life Among Aged Blacks." *The Family Coordinator* 21 (1972)21–27.

Jackson, Jacquelyne. Negro Aged and Social Gerontology, A Critical Evaluation." *Journal of Social and Behavioral Sciences* 13 (1968): 42–47.

Jackson, Jacquelyne J. "Negro Aged in North Carolina." *North Carolina Journal of Mental Health* 4 (1970) 43–52.

Jackson, Jacquelyne J. "Negro Aged parents and Adult Children: Their Affective Relationships." *Varia* (Spring Issue, 1969): 1–14.

Jackson, Jacquelyne J. "Negro Aged: Toward Needed Research in Social Gerontology." *The Gerontologist* 11 (1971): 52–57.

Jackson, Jacquelyne J. "Research, Training, Service, and Action Concerns About Black Aging and Aged Persons: An Overview." In *Proceedings of the Research Conference on Minority Group Aged in the South*, edited by Jacquelyne J. Jackson, pp. 41–47. Durham, North Carolina: Duke University, 1972.

Jackson, Jacquelyne J. "Sex and Social Class Variations in Black Adult Parent-Adult Child Relationships. *Aging and Human Development* 2 (1971): 96–107.

Jackson, Jacquelyne J. "Social Gerontology and the Negro: A Review." *The Gerontologist* 7 (1967): 168–78. Reprinted in *Sociological Symposium*, No. 2 (Spring 1969): 101 21.

Jackson, Jacquelyne J. and Ball, Mercerdee E. "A Comparison of Rural and Urban Georgia Aged Negroes." *Journal of the Association of Social Science Teachers* 12 (1966): 30–37.

Jackson, Jacquelyne J., and Davis, Abraham, Jr. "Characteristic Patterns of Aged, Rural Negroes in Macon County." In *A Survey of Selected Socioeconomic Characteristics of Macon County, Alabama, 1965*, edited by Beulah C. Johnson, pp. 122–57. Tuskegee, Alabama: Macon County Community Action Program Offices, 1966.

Jackson, Jacquelyne, ed. 1975. *Aging Black Women: Selected Readings for NCBA*. National Caucus on the Black Aged.

Jackson, Jacquelyne J., editor. *Proceedings of the Research Conference on Minority Group aged in the South*. Durham, North Carolina: Duke University, 1972.

Jackson, Jacquelyne. 1993, *The MTEARBE Black Church Manual on Eldercare for At-Risk Black Elders in Pitt County, North Carolina*. Raleigh, NC: Shaw Divinity School.

Jackson, Jacquelyne. November 29, 1994. "Social Security should be a true insurance program." *The Herald-Sun*. Durham, NC: A8.

Jackson, Jacquelyne. October 6, 1995. "Get over it, Herald-Sun." *The Herald–Sun*. Durham, NC: A12.

Jackson, Jacquelyne. 1 October 28, 1994, "Pitt County responded wisely to Few Gardens Killing." *The Herald-Sun*. Durham, NC: A12.

Jackson, Jacquelyne, October 16, 1994, "County has no mandate for full aid to nonprofits." *The Herald-Sun*. Durham, NC: A14.

Jet. June 6, 1994. "Dr. Joyce Ladner, Howard University Vice President, Named its New Acting President," p. 5. Johnson Publishing Company.

Jet. July 10, 1995. "Tickertape," p. 11. Johnson Publishing Company.

Kansas City Star. February 28, 1995. "Ethnic identities help women ease into older years: Strong cultural roles linked to positive reactions to aging," p. E 1. The Kansas City Star Company.

Karenga, Maulana. 1993. *Introduction to Afro-American Studies*. Los Angeles, California: The University of Sankore Press.

Kentucky Kernel. November 8, 1994, "Discrimination, low access hurt black youth."

Ladner, Joyce A. 1971. *Tomorrow's Tomorrow: The Black Woman*. Garden City, NY: Doubleday.

Ladner, Joyce A., ed. 1973. *The Death of White Sociology*. New York, NY: Random House.

Ladner, Joyce A. 1986. "Black Women Face the 21st Century: Major Issues and Problems." *The Black Scholar*, September/October.

Ladner, Joyce A. "Birmingham Funeral." *New American* 3 (1963): 2.

Ladner, Joyce A. 1964. "Intervention Strategy and Unemployment." St. Louis: Social Science Institute, Washington University.

Ladner, Joyce A. 1964 "Planned parenthood and Intervention Research." St. Louis: Social Science Institute, Washington University.

Ladner, Joyce A. "Racism and Comprehensive Planning." *Journal of the American Institute of Planners*. 35 (1969): 68–74.

Ladner, Joyce A. 1969. "What 'Black Power' Means to Negroes in Mississippi." *Trans-action* 5 (1967): 7–1 5. Reprinted in Blacks in the United States, edited by Norval D. Glenn and Charles M. Bonjean, pp. 444–57. San Francisco: Chandler Publishing Co.

Ladner, Joyce A. "White America's Response to Black Militancy." In *Black Americans*, edited by John F. Szwed, pp. 205–18. New York: Basic Books, 1970.

Ladner, Joyce A. "Women in Poverty: Its Roots and Effects." In *What Is Happening to American Women*, edited by Anne Scott. Atlanta: Southern Publishers Press, 1970.

Ladner, Joyce A. and Hammond, Boone E. 1969. "Socialization into Sexual Behavior." In *The Individual, Society, and Sex: Background Readings for Sex Educators*, edited by Carlfred Broderick and Jessie Bernard, pp. 41–52. Baltimore: Johns Hopkins University Press.

Ladner, Joyce A. and Stafford, Walter W. "Black Repression in the Cities." *The Black Scholar* 1 (1970): 38–52.

Lemert, Charles and Esme Bahn, eds. 1998. *The Voice of Anna Julia Cooper*. Boulder, Colorado: Rowman and Littlefield.

Lengermann, P. M. & Niebrugge-Brantley. 1998. *The Women Founders: Sociology and Social Theory, 1830–1930*. Boston: McGraw-Hill.

Mills, C. Wright. 1959. *The Sociological Imagination*. New York: Grove Press, Inc.

Myers, Lena Wright. 1991. *Black Women: Do They Cope Better*? San Francisco: Mellen Research University Press.

Newsweek, November 12, 1979. "Mississippi Revisited," p. 49.

Oppenheimer, Martin and Murray, Martin. 1988. *Critical Sociology*, vol. 15 no. 2, (Summer).

Rodgers-Rose, LaFrancis, ed. 1980. *The Black Woman*. Beverly Hills, CA/London: Sage Publications.

Rodgers-Rose, LaFrancis and Rodgers, James T. 1985. *Strategies for Resolving Conflict in Black Male-Female Relationships*. Plainfield, NJ: Traces Institute Publications.

Rose, LaFrances R. 1965. Interpersonal Relations Among School Children in an Iowa City. A Research Report of the Iowa Urban Community Research Center.

Sewell, William. 1992. "Some Observations and Reflections on the Role of Women and Minorities in the Democratization of the American Sociological Association," *The American Sociologist* 23 (Spring): 56–64.

The State Journal (1995) "Sociologist: Racial identification more than black-and-white issue." October 9, Frankfort, KY.

Turner, William. (2000). "Wrong Word," *Winston-Salem Journal*. Winston-Salem, N.C.

UK College of Arts and Sciences Distinguished Professor Lecture. Lexington, February 24, 1993.

Wells-Barnett, Ida B. 1987 [1892]. *On Lynchings*. Salem, New Hampshire: Ayer.

Harris, Trudier (ed.). 1991. *Selected Works of Ida B. Wells-Barnett*. New York: Oxford University Press.

Who's Who in America. 1984–85. 43rd ed. vol. 1.

Wilkinson, Doris. 1977. "The stigmatization process: The politicization of the Black male's identity." Pp. 145–148 in D. Wilkinson and R. Taylor (eds.). *The Black Male in America: Perspectives on his status in contemporary society*. Chicago: Nelson-Hall.

Wilkinson, Doris. 1980. Play Objects as tools of propaganda: Characterizations of the African American Male." *Journal of Black Psychology* 7: 1–16.

Wilkinson, Doris. 1995. "Gender and Social Inequality: the prevailing significance of race," *Daedalus: Journal of the American Academy of Arts and Sciences*, 124: 167–178.

Wilkinson, Doris. 2000. "Rethinking the Concept of 'Minority': A Task for Social Scientists and Practitioners." *Journal of Sociology and Social Welfare*, 27:115–132.

Wilkinson, Doris. 1989. "Revitalizing the American University: A Social Science Renaissance in Problem Solving." *Social Problems*, 36: 1–13.

Wilkinson, Doris. 1994. "Anti-Semitism and African Americans." *Society*. 31 (September/October): 45–48.

Wilkinson, Doris. 1987. "Transforming National Health Policy: The Significance of the Stratification System." *The American Sociologist* 18 (Summer):140–144.

Wilkinson, Doris. 1987. "The Doll Exhibit: A Psycho-Cultural Analysis of Black Female Role Stereotypes." *The Journal of Popular Culture*. 21 (Fall): 19–29.

Wilkinson, Doris. 2000. "Integration Dilemmas in a racist culture." In S. Steinberg (ed.) *Race and Ethnicity in the United States: Issues and Debates*. Boston: Blackwell Publishers, pp. 254–260.

Wilkinson, Doris. 1991. "The Segmented labor market and African American Women from 1890–1960: A Social History Interpretation." *Research in Race and Ethnic Relations*, 6.

Wilkinson, Doris. 1997. "Racism and Capitalism: The Critical Theories of Oliver Cox."*Research in Race and Ethnic Relations*, 10: 27–41.

Wilkinson, Doris and Gary King. 1987. "Conceptual and Methodological Issues in the Use of Race as a Variable: Policy Implications." *The Milbank Quarterly*. 65 (September): 56–71.

SELECTED WORKS BY AND ABOUT BLACK WOMEN

Berry, Mary Frances. 1983. "Blacks in Predominantly White Institutions of Higher Learning." *In State of Black America*, 1989, edited by James Williams, 295–318. New York: Urban League.

Cary, Lorene. 1991. *Black Ice*. New York: Alfred A. Knopf.

Collins, Patricia Hill.1998. *Fighting Words: Black Women and the Search for Justice*. Minneapolis: University of Minnesota Press.

———. 1990. *Black Feminist Thought: Knowledge, Consciousness and the Politics of Empowerment*. New York: Routledge.

Collins, Sharon. 1997. *Black Corporate Executives: The Making and Breaking of a Black Middle Class*. Philadelphia: Temple University Press.

Davis, Angela Y. 1974. *An Autobiography*. New York: Random House.

Dill, Bonnie Thornton. 1988. "Our Mothers' Grief: Racial Ethnic Women and the Maintenance of Families" *Journal of Family History* 13: 415–31.

———. 1980. "The Means to Put My Children Through: Childrearing Goals and Strategies among Black Female Domestic Servants." In *The Black Woman*, edited by Lafrancis Rodgers-Rose, 107–23. Beverly Hills, Calif.: Calif.: Sage Publications.

Essed, Philomena, 1990. *Everyday Racism: Reports from Women of Two Cultures*. Claremont, Calif.: Hunter House.

Fields, Barbara. 1990. "Slavery, Race, and Ideology in the United States of America." *New Left Review* 1981: 95–118.

Fleming, Jacqueline. 1985. *Blacks in Colleges: A Comparative Study of Student Success in Black and White Colleges*. San Francisco: Jossey-Bass.

Gibbs, Jewelle T. 1977. "Black Students in Integrated Colleges: Problems and Prospects." In *Black/Brown/White Relations*, edited by Charles Willie, 35–57. New Brunswick, N.J.: Transaction Books.

Higginbotham, Elizabeth. 1994. "Black Professional Women: Job Ceilings and Employment Sectors." In *Women of Color in U.S. Society*, edited by Maxine Baca Zinn and Bonnie Thornton Dill, 113–31. Philadelphia: Temple University Press.

Hine, Darlene Clark. 1989. *Black Women in White: Racial Conflict and Cooperation in the Nursing Profession*. Bloomington: Indiana University Press.

Jewell, Karen Sue. 1993. *From Mammy to Miss America and Beyond: Cultural Images and the Shaping of U.S. Policy*. New York: Routledge.

Lawrence-Lightfoot, Sara. 1994. *I've Known Rivers: Lives of Loss and Liberation*. Reading, Mass.: Addison-Wesley.

McAdoo, Harriette Pipes. 1997. "Upward Mobility across Generations of African American Families." In *Black Families*, 3rd ed., edited by H. P. McAdoo, 139–62. Thousand Oaks, Calif.: Sage Publications.

Marks, Carole. 1991. "The Urban Underclass," *Annual Review of Sociology* 17: 445–66.

Morton, Patricia. 1991. *Disfigured Images: The Historical assault on Afro-American Women*. New York: Praeger.

Shaw, Stephanie J.1996. *What a Woman Ought to Be and to Do: Black Professional Women Workers during the Jim Crow Era*. Chicago: University of Chicago Press.

Tatum, Beverly Daniel. 1997. "Why Are All the Black Kids Sitting Together in the Cafeteria?" *And Other Conversations about Race*. New York: Basic Books.

Tatum, Beverly Daniel. 1987. *Assimilation Blues: Black Families in a White Community*. New York: Greenwood Press.

Tucker, M. Belinda, and Claudia Mitchell-Kernan. 1996. *The Decline of Marriage among African Americans* (editors). New York: Russell Sage Foundation.

Index